LEADERSHIP...
Biblically Speaking

The Power of Principle-Based Leadership

DAVID COTTRELL

LEADERSHIP...
Biblically Speaking

Library of Congress Catalog Card Number: 98-93877
        Cottrell, R. David., 1953–
                Leadership . . . Biblically Speaking: The Power of Principle-Based
                Leadership/David Cottrell

Printed in the United States of America.

ISBN: 0-9762528-6-4
Published by: CornerStone Leadership
                        P.O. Box 764087
                        Dallas, Texas 75376
                        1-888-789-LEAD

Credits
Editors   Alice Adams
                                                   Tamara Jampo
Design, art direction, and production   Melissa Monogue, Back Porch Creative, Plano, TX
                                                   info@BackPorchCreative.com

This book is dedicated to the pastors who helped shape my life:

John Bisagno
H. D. McCarty
Glen Schmucker
Ken Story
Herb Pedersen
Bill White

And in memory of the person who most influenced my life as my pastor, friend, mentor and father:

Ralph Cottrell

And to all pastors who sacrifice their time, energy and love to further the kingdom of God.

Respect those who work hard among you,
who are over you in the Lord and who admonish you.
Hold them in the highest regard in love because of their work.
– I Thessalonians 5:12-13

TABLE OF CONTENTS

JACUZZIS, LADDERS AND THE CROSS

Whoever acknowledges me before men, I will also acknowledge him before my Father in heaven. But whoever disowns me before men, I will disown him before my Father in heaven.
– Matthew 10:32-33

I was a Jacuzzi Christian.

When being a Christian was relaxing, warm, soothing, massaging, bubbling, and without risk, I sat in the front pew. I was casually acquainted with God, enjoying the warm jet streams of idle conversations when Christianity was being discussed. I luxuriated in the soothing bubbles of Bible study and church attendance, but when being an active Christian became uncomfortable my response was, "Hey, I'm a Christian, but I'm not one of those radicals." I believed in the power, love and sovereignty of Jesus Christ, but to see that side of me you had to catch me on Sunday – not Monday through Saturday.

Yes, I was successful , by the world's standards, yet my life was empty. I was standing on the top rung of the corporate ladder with a cross hidden in my pocket ... but my ladder was propped against the wrong building ... a building made of pride, money and possession – not faith, hope a love.

Hiding my cross was my lack of commitment and total dedication to fulfill my purpose in the terms of God's will. I was successful, yet I felt like I was missing something.

The Bible says to take up your cross daily. I took up the cross only when it was convenient and without personal risk. I did not truly understand the meaning of *"For the wisdom of this world is foolishness in God's sight."*[1]

Then one day I realized I could make a difference in the lives of others. I was reading Patrick Morley's introduction in *The Seven Seasons of a Man's Life,* where he speaks of the shortness of our life on earth and what we do with the time we have.

If I live to be 80, my tombstone will read 1953 – 2033. Morley's question was, "What will you do with the dash?"

Think about it. It's a good question.

This book offers a practical blueprint to add value to your own dash – by enriching your leadership style with biblical direction and answering some fundamental questions faced by Christian leaders. Questions like how can Christian leaders succeed in a world where success is judged by the worth of possessions we accumulate? How can we live for Jesus and be driven by profits at the same time? What leadership principles cannot be compromised by a Christian leader?

All of these questions are answered in the Bible and are addressed in this book.

While reading this book, you will discover the leadership principles expressed in the Old and New Testaments are just as applicable today as in the time of Moses, David, Job, Jesus, Peter and Paul. These principles apply to how we lead in business, church, school and our homes. They are self-evident, self-validating and enduring principles of human relations taught throughout the Bible – and they work!

We are all leaders and when we lead, we influence others. The Bible provides explicit direction on how to influence others: *"For we are God's workmanship, created in Christ Jesus to do good works, which God prepared in advance for us to do."*[2]

Today's workplace continues to be a fertile mission field and all Believers are missionaries. In Ephesians 4:1, Paul wrote, *"I urge you to live a life worthy of the calling you have received."*

As we go through our workweek, we are presented with scores of opportunities to share our faith through our words and actions. Nothing is more important.

I encourage you to use this book as a guide to help you get out of your Jacuzzi, prop your ladder against the appropriate building, get the cross out of your pocket and prepare to serve!

*If anyone would come after me, he must deny himself
and take up his cross daily and follow me.*
— Luke 9:23

CHAPTER ONE

THE CALL FOR LEADERSHIP

I have indeed seen the misery of my people in Egypt. I have heard them crying
out because of their slave drivers, and I am concerned about their suffering.
— Exodus 3:7

So now I am sending you to Pharaoh to bring my people the Israelites out of Egypt.
— Exodus 3:10

God's call for Christian leaders today carries the same urgency as His call to Moses more than 3,000 years ago. America needs Christian leaders to make a difference in our businesses, churches, schools and homes.

Many Christians are hesitant to share the Good News of Christ because of the same reasons Moses was reluctant to lead the Israelites. They may not feel qualified or trained, or they may not be willing to accept the risk. The result? There is little or no difference between the actions of Christian leaders and those of non-Christians.

Here's something to think about: Our situation today is strikingly similar to the time when God called Moses to lead the Israelites out of the wilderness in about 1450 B.C.[1] Now, as then, people are miserable. They are crying out, and God is concerned because He loves us.

The message is this: America needs integrity-based leaders!

Surveys reveal the following about attitudes toward leaders:

- Only 14 percent of leaders are seen by their followers as people they would choose as role models.[2]

- Less than 50 percent of people trust their leaders.[3] Trust is a basic requirement for effective leadership. Does it matter how well you communicate or how clear your mission statement if people do not trust what you say? How do you follow someone you cannot trust?

- Sixty-one percent of today's business leaders do not exhibit appropriate managerial behavior.[4] Whether it is lack of communication, confusing direction, lack of recognition, sexual or verbal harassment, or simply not doing anything, six out of ten are not effective leaders.

- Forty percent of employees said their leaders do a poor job of solving problems.[5] The purpose of the leader is to clear a path for people to be successful in accomplishing a goal. If you can't solve problems, you can't effectively lead people.

- Fifty percent said their leaders tolerate poor performance too long.[6] People want to be a part of a winning team, yet one-half of those surveyed felt their teammates were hindering the team's performance.

- Forty percent of leaders are threatened by talented subordinates.[7] The best leaders hire the most talented people. They search for people with high intellect, experience, and the right personality to help them accomplish their goals.

Because of these attitudes, today's employees are demonstrating their dissatisfaction by being disloyal to their leaders and organizations. Many say, "I'll stay here until a better offer comes along."

But employees aren't the only problem. On average, U.S. corporations are now losing half their customers in five years, half their employees in four years, and half their investors in less than one year. Growing and widespread disloyalty is stunting corporate performance by 25 to 50 percent.[8]

The cost of ineffective leadership is staggering, but the problem doesn't stop there. Investor turnover creates a constant "do it now" mentality. The present quarter's profit is the only measurement that matters – a short-term focus that creates long-term problems. The fastest way to show quick profit? Cut people, cut training, increase profits, cash in and move on to the next deal.

In addition to the unrest created by mergers, layoffs and cutbacks, front-line and mid-level managers are thrown into battle without sufficient training or experience. Many companies spend more resources developing a mission statement than they do developing strong leaders. In fact, some spend more money framing the mission statement than they do equipping their leaders for success.

Just as in the time of Moses, people today need strong and courageous leaders. The Book of Exodus provides descriptions that could easily fit our society today:

"I have indeed seen the misery of my people in Egypt."

♦ ***People Are Miserable.*** More than 50,000 people quit their jobs every day. They want their leaders to recognize the contributions they are making every day. Most people do not quit jobs because of pay, benefits, or vacation plans … they quit their leader!

People quit people long before they quit organizations. Most of the time, they quit leaders because the leader has lost touch with the team and the leader's ego runs rampant. Nothing destroys people or organizations more quickly than leaders with out of control egos.

Biblically-based leadership is servant leadership – recognizing that the leader needs his team at least as much as the team needs the leader.

"I have heard them crying out because of their slave drivers."

♦ *People Are Crying Out.* The stress experienced in all areas of life today is a reflection of people searching for the truth. Employees are frustrated and are likely to transfer their frustration to their associates. Students are turning to alcohol and drugs to overcome feelings of inadequacy. All are seeking leaders of integrity and trust; leaders who are Christian role models in all areas of their lives.

"I am concerned about their suffering."

♦ *God Is Concerned About Our Suffering.* There are two common denominators in today's world. God loves all of us and we all suffer.

Many times we look at people we admire and assume they have no reason to suffer. They have money, friends, influence – everything we think eliminates suffering, and we sometimes make it a personal goal to walk in their shoes. The fact is that no one is immune to pain and suffering. If you were able to walk in anyone else's shoes, you would find that the other person is facing challenges similar to your own.

The question is *why* do we suffer? Do we suffer because of the kingdom of God or do we suffer because of bad choices we make because of our nature to sin?

King David suffered for the kingdom of God as well as his poor choices. As God's chosen and anointed leader, David was not allowed to accept his leadership position. Instead, he was cast out to scrounge for food and shelter – a time of "righteous suffering," suffering within God's direction. Then, much later in his life, when David chose to change his focus from God's plan to his personal plan, worldly desires and disaster resulted.

God does love us! To suffer for the cross is worthwhile, but to suffer for worldly goals is opposed to God's will and purpose.

THE PRICE OF LEADERSHIP

As with anything of value, you will pay a price to become an effective leader. Leaving your comfort zone, accepting additional responsibilities, and being held accountable for your actions and the actions of others are part of that price.

Moses knew the price God was asking him to pay.

Imagine how Moses felt when God announced he had chosen him to be the leader? "Me? Lead your people? Ha! I am just a shepherd. I am perfectly content to tend my father-in-law's flock. The sheep don't talk back. I get them where they need to go by using this staff, and they never complain. I enjoy what I do. It doesn't take much effort. I just lead sheep. I don't want to take the risk of leading the people. Besides, I don't think I would be any good at it, anyway."

He also might have said, "Okay, I need to convince God I'm not the guy for this job. Maybe he'll show some mercy and release me from this leading-his-people concept."

We're no different from Moses. We have our comfort zones – and so did he – so much so, he was reluctant to take a risk. Leading the Israelites would mean a change, and just as it was then, change is uncomfortable.

In his efforts to wiggle out of this overwhelming request from God, Moses came up with five lame excuses:[9]

♦ **Lord, I Am Not Qualified.** "I am just a homeboy shepherd tending sheep for my father-in-law. I've never led people anywhere, and besides, that's an awesome responsibility." Few of us accept the responsibility of leadership without being overwhelmed and frightened.

God answered Moses' objection with the simple statement: *"I will be with you."* Then God gave a vision of the end result: *"When you have brought the people out of Egypt, you will worship God on this mountain."*

Moses may have answered, "When I have brought the people out of Egypt? Wait, I am not through with my argument. That was just my first objection." And like us, he was ready with another excuse:

♦ **But, Lord, I Am Not Trained.** Moses felt unprepared for a leadership role. He didn't realize God had been preparing him throughout his life. He had been an Egyptian prince with everything done for him. Now he was a shepherd and had no one to do anything for him.

God answered his objection: *"Say I am who I am. I am sent me to you."* Once again God looked to the future and told Moses what would happen: *"The elders of Israel will listen to you."*

If your path is God's will, He provides for your needs.

♦ Moses' next strategy was to personalize the risk: **But Lord, This Is a Risk for You and Me.** By this time Moses must have had some clue that his excuses weren't working, so he tried to spread the risk to include God. *"What if they do not believe me or listen?"*

God answered with undeniable proof that Moses was the right person for the job, changing Moses' staff to a snake, making Moses' hand leprous, and then restoring both.

All changes in jobs, responsibilities, business and life itself involve risks. What are these risks? Looking foolish, making bad decisions, losing pride, and being held to a higher standard … for starters. Leaders have far more exposure to risk than followers, but the greater risk is *not* following God's call for us.

All Christians are commanded to be leaders, regardless of their job titles or responsibilities. Refusing to respond to God's call makes them miserable until they accept the risk and trust God to provide.

♦ Then Moses delivered the mother of all excuses, the excuse he thought could not be overcome: **But, Lord, I Physically Can't Do It.** Moses was feeling the way many of us feel about the demands of leadership. By accepting leadership positions we, like Moses, may face long days, working weekends and excessive travel along with an overwhelming number of speeches, continual relocations and other personal hardships.

Moses had another good reason – *"I am slow of speech and tongue."*

You have to admit – that was a good excuse! Moses was not a good communicator, and he knew good verbal communication is basic equipment if you're going to be a strong leader. Imagine his discomfort! He had been leading sheep, not dealing with people.

One of the greatest sources of stress today comes when you have to address a group. Either you have the talent to speak in public or you don't. Moses didn't.

But, once again God provided the answer. Instead of healing Moses' slow tongue, God sent Aaron to be Moses' spokesman.

Isn't it interesting that God chose to change a staff to a snake and to make a hand leprous and restored, yet chose not to heal Moses' slowness of speech?

Without a doubt, God could have made Moses an eloquent, strong communicator to lead His people. Instead, Moses was like all of us with weaknesses God used to make him a better person and leader. The lesson for today's leaders is the same: admit your weaknesses and surround yourself with talented people who can complement your weaknesses.

♦ But **Lord, Please Send Someone Else.** By this time Moses was desperate. He had used all of his excuses and God had overcome every obstacle, but Moses tried last appeal to God: *"O Lord, please send someone else to do it."* Moses was begging for someone else – anyone else – to be the chosen leader. He still was not confident that he could do the job because he was looking at the challenge from **his** perspective. God was looking at Moses from a different perspective and was totally confident.

"Take your staff and go!" God said. You are the man. You are God's man!

Out of excuses, Moses finally resigned his shepherd job and obeyed the Lord! Then … *"Moses and Aaron brought together all the elders of the Israelites, and Aaron told them everything the Lord said to Moses. He also performed the signs before the people, and they believed. And when they heard that the Lord was concerned about them and had seen their misery, they bowed down and worshiped."*[10]

SUMMARY

God continues to call us to be leaders; leaders who are imperfect, unsure of ourselves, untrained, afraid of failure and unable to understand why God has called us to lead. God calls CEOs, vice presidents, supervisors, team leaders, individual contributors, schoolteachers, principals, students, husbands, wives, sons and daughters and pastors to be leaders. **Leadership is not something that is done by people in high places … it is done by people in all kinds of roles. Wherever you are called to work, you are also called to lead.**

Waiting for perfect conditions?

Won't happen. As the Bible says, *"Whoever watches the wind will not plant; whoever looks at the clouds will not reap."*[11] Don't wait on conditions to be perfect before trusting God's direction. Accept the challenge and respond to the call for leadership in your chosen field.

No temptation has seized you except what is common to man.
And God is faithful; he will not let you be tempted beyond
what you can bear. But when you are tempted, he will also provide
a way out so that you can stand up under it.
– I Corinthians 10:13

PART ONE

THE VALUES PRINCIPLES

INTEGRITY ◆ RESPONSIBILITY
COMMITMENT ◆ VISION

Everything begins with the values principles. Do I trust you?
Will you allow me to accept my responsibility?
Are you committed enough for me to risk my commitment?
Do I know where we are going and why?

The values principles are the foundation of leadership.

CHAPTER TWO

INTEGRITY

My lips shall not speak wickedness, nor my tongue utter deceit.
— Job 27:4

THE PRINCIPLE OF INTEGRITY

**Leadership results improve in proportion
to the level of trust earned by the leader.**

When asked which leadership trait, in a list of sixteen, has the single greatest impact on an executive's effectiveness, 71 percent of the 2,300 executives surveyed listed integrity at the top.[1]

Think about it. How difficult it is to get 71 percent of senior executives to agree on ANYTHING – especially when there are fifteen other choices?

The participants in that study know the same thing you and I know. If the leader has sacrificed integrity, nothing else really matters.

♦ Does it matter how often you communicate with your people if they do not trust you?

♦ Does it matter how committed you are, what mission statement you've developed, how optimistic you are, how skilled you are at resolving conflicts, or how courageous you are if your followers do not trust you?

None of these leadership traits really matter if your integrity is continually questioned by your followers.

Leaders who have integrity possess one of the most respected virtues in life. If you can be trusted, whether alone or in a crowd, and if you are truly a person of your word and convictions, then you are fast becoming a unique and valued person.

Integrity is the cornerstone of leadership!

People want leaders whose audio (words) is in sync with their video (actions), have earned their team's commitment and have proven to be honest and trustworthy. People are searching for leaders whose values are consistent and do not change based on daily situations.

Sounds pretty simple, right? Yet a leader's sacrifice of integrity is the principal reason people look for someone else to follow. Judgment errors may be forgiven and forgotten, but mistakes of integrity are always remembered.

WHAT IS INTEGRITY?

The dictionary says integrity is the rigid adherence to a code of behavior which can be measured only by a person's actions.

Your spouse may say integrity is total commitment and loyalty. Your team may say that it is doing what you say you will do. Your investors may define integrity as finding no surprises in your financials. Your friends probably say it is just being who you are.

Regardless of who describes it, integrity is a by-product of trust, which is a by-product of honesty. A deficit in trust and honesty can cost organizations millions of dollars in sales and profits. When people lose faith in their leader – productivity, job satisfaction and morale all suffer.

HOW IMPORTANT IS INTEGRITY?

In our warp-speed world of computer technology, when you install a new software program on your computer it will automatically run what is called an "integrity check" – a series of tests to determine if any part of the program has been lost or damaged. If any piece of the code in that program doesn't have complete integrity, the program as a whole can't be trusted. At best, you would have a program that wasn't functioning properly. At worst, using a program lacking integrity could cause you to lose valuable data or even damage your computer. So, the integrity check is vital.

But as the pace of business gains even more speed (thanks, in part, to the integrity of our computer programs), we are paying less attention to personal integrity. Here's an example: When it is discovered that a politician lacks integrity, we aren't surprised. In fact, we actually expect it.

Closer to home, many people are encouraged to do "whatever it takes" to claw their way to the top and ignore personal and Biblical principles in favor of the big house in the gated community, the BMW and the Rolex. Some business leaders don't think twice about lying to get their point across. And unfortunately, these so-called white lies accompanied with short cuts and "stretching the truth" are commonplace in our boardrooms ... and often our bedrooms.

This lack of integrity in Christian leaders causes nonbelievers to become skeptical and turn away from Christianity. God's standard for integrity in every leader is living a walk and talking the talk that resembles the conduct of Jesus Christ. There is no gray area.

Integrity is the principle leadership trait for long-term, positive results.

Psalm 15 defines integrity and explains the results of a life of integrity:

> *"Lord, who may dwell in your sanctuary? Who may live on your holy hill? He whose walk is **blameless** and who does what is **righteous**, who speaks the **truth** from his heart and has **no slander** on his tongue, who does his neighbor **no wrong** and casts **no slur** on his fellowman, who despises a vile man but **honors those who fear the Lord**, who **keeps his oath** even when it hurts, who lends his money without usury and does not accept a bribe against the innocent. He who does these things will never be shaken."*

Can you imagine the pleasure of working with people who fit this description?

A blameless, righteous, truthful person who always keeps promises, who always does the right thing (even when it hurts), is the type of person we want to be. This is also the leader people want to follow.

The Bible describes many who would not sacrifice their integrity, even when it hurt:

♦ Jacob instructed Joseph's brothers to return the money they had mistakenly brought back from Egypt. Even though the money was taken by mistake and was not stolen, the message was clear – do the right thing and return what is not yours![2]

♦ Job's integrity was constantly challenged, and he withstood the test. Job knew that his code of behavior was to honor God, and he never wavered in that conviction. After losing his flock, Job blessed the name of the Lord. When in such physical pain that even his friends did not recognize him, Job blessed the Lord. When his friends questioned his loyalty to God, Job honored God. Job never wavered in his integrity, and God blessed him many times over.[3]

♦ David spoke of integrity protecting him. In Psalm 25:21 he wrote, *"May integrity and uprightness protect me, because my hope is in you."* Integrity protects us from the slippery slope of telling one small lie that leads to another lie.

THE INTEGRITY GAP

There is a huge gap between the world's standard for integrity and God's standard. This becomes increasingly clear every day. God's standard is to do what is right, regardless of the consequences.

Paul wrote, *"Do not be overcome by evil, but overcome evil with good."*[4] The world's standard is to do what is right when it is convenient, or if you think your chances of getting caught are slim.

Christian leaders cannot straddle this growing integrity gap. It is either one side or the other, and you have to be consistent.

Developing trust depends entirely upon the integrity you consistently demonstrate. But, how often have you seen leaders spending more time polishing their image than protecting their integrity? They were more concerned with how they looked or sounded than with what they were doing.

Who are they trying to fool? Leaders are ultimately judged on their actions, not their image.

EVERYTHING COUNTS

Some people would like to think that what they do really doesn't matter. And, what difference does it really make if you sacrifice your personal values for values that are accepted by the world as normal? It makes a big difference because people are watching us, and everything we do makes a statement of which side of the integrity gap we are standing.

Former University of Florida quarterback Danny Wuerffel is no Playboy, at least not a member of Playboy Magazine's prestigious all-American college pre-season football team. A devout Christian and son of an Air Force minister, Danny declined an invitation to be named the controversial magazine's National Scholar Athlete of the Year. "It didn't take any thought at all," said Wuerffel. "It would've been a lot of fun, and I'm sure there's a good bit of the population out there that would think I'm silly for doing this. But, there's also a good bit of the population that would understand that's not the type of person I would want to portray myself as.'

IMAGE VS. CHARACTER

Think of yourself as an iceberg. People see what is above the water – your image and personality. Unseen is the much larger, greater and more powerful foundation below the water level - your character and integrity. People can immediately judge a leader's personality and image because that is what they see. Character and integrity can usually be judged *only* through trials and experiences.

But, the speed of our communications – thanks to the Internet, cell phones, Blackberries and Wi-Fi technology – now make it possible to get below the waterline on most individuals much faster than ever before, particularly high profile individuals. Think about those individuals seemingly pristine in their image and on their resumes, who are quickly found (thanks to television sound bites and Internet research) to be less honorable than they appeared.

Ultimately, whether you're high profile or invisible, your integrity will eventually be tested. But, before the test, you must decide the price you are willing to pay to follow God's standard of doing the right thing … even if it hurts.

Here's one more factor to consider: The greater your responsibilities, the more your integrity will be exposed.

As you make decisions, you will be judged less on your image and more on the consistency of your character. **You should guard your integrity as you would guard your most valued treasures because that is exactly what it is!**

INTEGRITY IN THE NEWS
It is no secret that integrity has become a critical concern within today's business community. Read the paper or watch the evening news, and you find more than ample evidence that there are some serious problems with corporate as well as individual integrity.

Unfortunately, lack of integrity among our leaders has become so prevalent that many have become calloused to the news. Lack of integrity is becoming an accepted norm in everybody's eyes … except God's.

You have seen the headlines:

- ♦ Campaign funds misappropriated and raised illegally.

♦ Evangelist goes to prison for income tax evasion.

♦ Investors convicted of insider trading of company stock.

♦ Surprise witness confirms sexual abuse allegations.

♦ A major university declares 70 athletes ineligible and forfeits games.

♦ Executive loses multimillion dollar job because of expense account fraud.

Several years ago, one in every three city workers in Miami had filed for workers' compensation or disability. One hundred and twenty-three workers received workers' compensation for falling out of or into chairs. Ninety were injured by desks, fifteen were sidelined by lifting a TV or watching television, seven were disabled by paper cuts and two by candy.[5]

In another major city, the superintendent of schools – with the mission of protecting and training our children – pleaded guilty to embezzlement to avoid other charges. She had embezzled taxpayers' dollars to furnish a room in her house, causing her to lose her $200,000-a-year job because she sacrificed her integrity for $16,000 worth of furniture. At her sentencing the judge stated, "You had this trust, and you violated that in a blatant way. It almost looks like an arrogant abuse of power."

What a price to pay! She lost everything she had worked for in her life, including the trust of thousands of people ... not to mention the children. Such trust will not be given to the next superintendent, or anyone else in that school district, for a long, long time.

INTEGRITY OUT OF THE NEWS

It is easy to criticize these obvious mistakes in integrity, but before we cast stones we may want to check ourselves. Integrity mistakes happen all around us, and most of the time those mistakes never make the news. Consider these situations:

♦ Padding the expense account to cover "miscellaneous expenses"

♦ Taking office supplies from work because "they overbought anyway"

♦ Making long-distance calls at work because "they can't track them"

♦ Stretching the truth to get an order

♦ Not returning phone calls

♦ Copying software from work to use at home

♦ Being "out of the office" when you are really in the office

♦ Using company time and computers to order personal gifts online

♦ Using "I didn't receive the message" as an excuse for your lack of action

"But, those actions are so minor," you may be saying. Or you may be thinking, "No big deal. Everybody does that stuff."

Yet, it is just this kind of "stuff" that chips away at your personal integrity, and by example, you are leading the people you influence to justify the same minor lies. Here's why – **even when you are not paying attention you are influencing other people. Yes, people are watching you – you are always leading. You have no choice about being a role model for others … the only choice you have is which role you will model.**

You are also a strong influence on the thoughts and behaviors of all the people around you – perhaps much stronger than you think. By virtue of having this influence, one of your most critical responsibilities is to model the behavior you expect from others, but remember this – you only earn the right to expect others to live with integrity by having the courage to become an integrity champion yourself.

ONE DEGREE AT A TIME

Most people do not make a conscious decision to sacrifice their integrity by making one big, bad mistake. It is the accumulation of bad choices, all of which seem minor, that lead to the next bad choice.

It is like the story of how to boil a frog. If you throw a frog into a pot of boiling water, he will leap out immediately because he realizes the danger and knows that he does not want to be in boiling water. Yet, if you put the same frog in a pot of cold water and slowly turn up the heat, the frog will never recognize the subtle changes in temperature and will remain in the pot until it reaches 212 degrees – boiling. If allowed, he would stay in the pot until he is boiled to well done!

That's how integrity is lost – one degree of dishonesty at a time – and the loser is not even aware of the severity of their situation.

God has always held Christian leaders to a standard of absolute integrity. In biblical times, God knew the great leaders could be trusted completely, regardless of the situation, whether anyone was around or not. God expects the same from us, but maintaining integrity is a continual challenge for all Christians.

Even the Apostle Paul wrestled with his integrity. See if this sounds familiar:

"For I have the desire to do what is good, but I cannot carry it out. For what I do is not the good I want to do; no, the evil I do not want to do – that I keep on doing."[6]

A leader without integrity who is followed because of his looks, perceived power, a recent speech or a charismatic personality is a leader who will be successful for only a short period of time. The leader who is consistent in his code of behavior will have committed followers. The Bible says, *"Blessed is the man who perseveres under trial, because when he has stood the test, he will receive the crown of life that God has promised to those that love him."*[7] Proverbs 10:9 says, *"The man of integrity walks securely, but he who takes crooked paths will be found out."* We cannot escape the accountability of our integrity.

PROTECTING INTEGRITY

There are five pillars of integrity for the Christian leader. Each is based on biblical values. Failure to adhere to any of the five will destroy confidence and trust in your leadership:

1. ***Keep your promises and promise only what you can deliver.*** It may sound simple, but a mistake many leaders make is overcommitting or committing to something beyond their control. Living up to your commitments is one of the principal ways your integrity is judged.

2. ***Stand up and speak out for what you believe.*** Your integrity begins when you speak out about what you believe. What are your core values? What is so important that it will never be compromised for any reason?

   Never leave people guessing about how you feel or where you stand. Understand exactly what you believe and communicate those beliefs without hesitation. If your beliefs and values are biblically based, they will never change.

3. *Always err on the side of fairness.* When you are involved in a gray area, err on the side of fairness. What you do is being watched by your team, and their judgments are made on *their* perception. It may not be fair, but you have to manage your people's perceptions and not all decisions are black or white. If there is a gray area, make the decision to err on the side of your follower. Swallowing pride is a small price to pay to retain or gain their trust in you.

4. *Live what you teach.* People are listening to what you say and watching the way you deliver the message, but they react to what they see you do. You can't fake what you teach. Walk your talk!

5. *Do what you say you will do.* The ultimate test of your integrity is if you do what you say you will do. Your word and your commitment are judged every time you say you are going to do something—regardless of how insignificant you consider the commitment.

In Matthew 5:37, Jesus taught us to *"Simply let your 'Yes' be 'Yes,' and your 'No' be 'No'; anything beyond this comes from the evil one."* Be reliable in honoring your commitments and promises. If the situation dictates a change and you are unable to live up to your word, communicate the reason thoroughly, honestly and quickly to minimize the damage.

Although none of the following actions are wrong or immoral and may be business necessities, they are easily questioned by others and may put your integrity at risk:

♦ Taking business trips with your secretary

♦ Socializing outside work with an associate in a compromising place

♦ Meeting someone of the opposite sex alone over dinner

♦ Consistently working late and alone with a business partner or colleague of the opposite sex

Be careful. Paul instructed Titus not to put himself in a position where his integrity could be questioned, *"In everything set them an example by doing what is good. In your teaching show integrity, seriousness and soundness of speech that cannot be condemned, **so that those who oppose you may be ashamed** because they have nothing bad to say about us."*[8] When your integrity is sacrificed or even questioned for any reason, there is a huge price to pay for its recovery.

SUMMARY
People may forgive and forget judgment errors, but will not forget integrity mistakes.

Business is personal. People commit themselves to other people, more than to an organization. If people don't trust the messenger, they won't buy into the message. Leadership begins with the leader's integrity. Without integrity, trust doesn't exist. Without trust, nothing else really matters.

Integrity is not just being fiscally trustworthy or handling issues in an exemplary and truthful fashion. Integrity is the commitment to do what is right regardless of the circumstance – no hidden agendas, no political games – do what is right! The Bible says, *"Even if you should suffer for what is right, you are blessed."*[9]

"Hold yourself responsible for a higher standard than anybody else expects of you. Never excuse yourself."
–Henry Ward Beecher

CHAPTER THREE

RESPONSIBILITY

From everyone who has been given much, much will be demanded;
and from the one who has been entrusted with much, much more will be asked.
— Luke 12:48

THE PRINCIPLE OF RESPONSIBILITY

Leadership results improve dramatically when the leader and his team accept total responsibility for their actions.

"**S**ome assembly required."

What those dreaded words really mean to me is, "Some parts left over, frustration ahead, and you will never get it put together correctly. Ha, ha, ha."

When I have to assemble something like a bicycle, it normally goes like this: I open the box and place the parts all over the garage floor. I briefly glance at the instruction book. Then I lay the book down because "I can figure this out." Several hours and two aspirin later, my task is completed. The bike is together. It has two tires, and my son Michael is thrilled as he rides down the sidewalk and "I'm the man!"

What difference does it make that I have six nuts and bolts remaining? No big deal. I am sure someone simply packed too many nuts and bolts. I put them in a growing collection of dribs and drabs marked, "Extra parts."

Several weeks later, the bike begins to wobble. I try to fix it, but I can't get the wheels to roll safely. I get a little upset because they just don't make bikes like they used to.

Within hours this new, expensive bike has become just another piece of worthless junk taking up space in my already crowded garage. I blame the bicycle manufacturer because I am sure there is no quality control in its assembly line.

Then, my handyman neighbor comes over, gets into my extra parts, finds the six missing nuts and bolts and fixes the bike – and it runs like a champ! The problem was that I did not accept the responsibility to follow the directions.

It is easy and sometimes satisfying to blame others, but the bike did not work because I failed to assemble the bike as instructed. Once I accepted that fact and got my neighbor to fix my problem, I quit blaming everyone else, stop making excuses and learned from my mistake.

EXCUSES – ALWAYS AN ABUNDANT SUPPLY

Sometimes responsibility is difficult for us to accept. Remember how Adam responded when God questioned him about who had eaten the forbidden fruit? He had an excuse. And then Eve's response was another excuse. Since the beginning of time, even though few people enjoy listening to them, we have had an abundant supply of excuses.

Several years ago, a radio series about honesty in America talked about excuses. "There are three types of excuses we use when we are accused of wrong doing," the commentator said. The first is outright denial a rejection of any involvement. Sometimes this is done even though the person is obviously guilty. The second is the "It's not my fault" excuse. The person looks around for someone he can blame. (Often it is a loved one – a husband, wife or parent. Sometimes it's the boss.) A third form of excuse is the "I did it, but ..." approach. In this instance, the person blames circumstances for his shortcoming. He's been struggling with some family problems, the assignment wasn't clear, the car's been giving him trouble, the weather was at fault or a myriad of other excuses.

Blaming other people or things is not a good long-term solution. No one likes hearing, "It is not my fault," "If they had done what they said, then I would have done what I was supposed to do," "I was too early," "I was too late," "I was too busy," or "It was El Niño."

You get the point.

THE NO-FAULT GENERATION

Have we forgotten to teach honesty and responsibility?

Take a few minutes to watch little children at play. Somebody ends up crying, but even before the wounded can report to Mom for treatment, somebody else is yelling, "But I didn't do anything! It wasn't me! It's not my fault!"

Is it in our DNA – this habit of blaming others, this inability to accept responsibility, to be accountable?

When did this epidemic of rejecting responsibility begin?

Was it during the Vietnam War? Was it after the "Twinkie defense," when the murderer of San Francisco Mayor George Moscone was given leeway because his depression was blamed on eating too many Twinkies? Was it when being a victim made "losers" the darling of daytime TV and "The Maury Povich Show?"

Follow the proceedings of any criminal trial.

He was caught with the murder weapon, but his attorney justifies that he was abused as a child. Her shoplifting was witnessed by several, but she's the product of a broken home. He has untreated attention deficit hyperactive syndrome. Her mother didn't love her. He grew up in a rough neighborhood. He was bullied in school.

In business, it's much the same: "My department has been hit with turnover so we didn't meet our deadline," "We just can't find people who want to work," or "It's the economy, stupid!"

Excuses, excuses.

But, it seems we Americans have become especially good at making excuses to avoid responsibility for our actions. We make excuses for things we did wrong, times we failed, things we don't want to do, situations we don't want to be in. How many times have you told someone "I forgot" when in reality you just didn't want to do what was asked in the first place?

Whatever happened to "The Buck Stops Here?"

Making excuses rather than accepting responsibility for your actions will destroy your effectiveness as a leader. You are not chosen to fill a position – you are chosen to fill a responsibility. Nobody needs a leader to find excuses and others to blame for failures.

As a Christian leader, your role is to avoid the temptation to fix the blame and, instead, search for ways to solve issues. Accepting responsibility is the first step toward the future. Making excuses and blaming others incarcerates us to live in the past.

A CULTURAL PROBLEM?

We can all take a lesson from the Japanese culture. When an error is made, the first step is to fix the problem, to resolve the issue. In American culture the first step toward resolving the problem is finding someone to blame, then we look to see if we can fix the problem.

Why do we find ourselves in this rut? Why do businesses remain broken even when the culprit is fired?

The answer is an easy one. Assuming responsibility can be a scary thing to do. However, for strong leaders, it's mandatory – and it is our responsibility to find solutions, not make excuses.

As Christian leaders, we have to answer for our actions and often the actions of others. That's why it's so tempting to make excuses and shirk responsibility … that's why it takes courage to accept it.

But, it ultimately leads to calmness, confidence and self-control – all qualities a strong leader needs to be effective.

The Bible is clear about our responsibility: *"Nothing in all creation is hidden from God's sight. **Everything is uncovered** and lay bare before the eyes of him to whom we must give account."*[1]

Ultimately, we will have to account for the way we deal with our responsibilities in each area of our lives. We are responsible for our relationships with our families and work associates, our finances, our health, and we are responsible for providing good role models to our children, our friends and our employees.

Jesus taught responsibility in a parable about loaned money.[2] As the story goes, the master divided talents among his servants according to their abilities. Of the three men given talents, the man who received the most talents accepted his responsibility, put the talents to work and gained more. Another man was given fewer talents, but accepted his responsibility and put his talents to work to gain more. The third man dug a hole in the ground, hid his talent and chose not to accept his responsibility of putting the talent to work. The two who accepted their responsibility were described as good and faithful. The one who did not was described as wicked and lazy, and he lost the talent he had been given.

Regardless of our talents, we are all responsible for being good stewards of our God-given abilities. The issue is not how much we have, but what we do with what we have.

LEADERSHIP ACCOUNTABILITY

Along with accepting responsibility comes the realization that the leader's standard for accountability is at a higher level than that of his followers. James taught about the accountability of leadership: *"Not many of you should presume to be teachers, my brothers, because you know that we who teach will be judged more strictly."*[3]

But, what about today's faith-based leaders? Aren't they different?

Ultimately everyone will be held accountable for their actions, but the exposure of leaders' sin impacts the lives of many people. Think about the well-known Christian leaders accused of embezzlement, greed and adultery. Each one had a negative impact on the cause of Christianity because of the influence the exposure of their sins had on others.

In addition to a higher standard of accountability, many of the rights evaporate as your responsibilities and your position is elevated.

♦ You no longer have the right to blame others for mistakes – you are responsible.

♦ You no longer have the right to be negative or cynical – you are responsible.

♦ You no longer have the right to avoid issues and not solve problems – you are responsible.

♦ You no longer have the right to choose to not make a decision – you are responsible.

Your responsibility cannot be avoided!

So, what are you responsible for at work? The actions of your team? Your boss? Your peers?

The answer is this: You are responsible for everything you control!

You control:

♦ Setting the standards for your work group's performance

♦ Providing your team feedback so they can improve and accept more responsibility

♦ Providing an atmosphere of truth and honesty

♦ Addressing – not ignoring – employee issues

♦ Giving your boss the positive and/or negative truth

♦ Providing input to your peers

♦ Building self- esteem in others

♦ Living a life worthy of following

You also control your choice of making excuses, complaining, or criticizing.

Most people go to work to do a good job. They perform at different levels, but they are there to do their best.

The former president of Hyatt Hotels once pointed out, "If there is anything I have learned in my 27 years in the service industry, it is this: 99 percent of all employees want to do a good job. How they perform is simply a reflection of the one for whom they work."[4]

In other words, the responsibility for the success of the team falls directly on the leader.

There are three major areas of a principle-based leader's responsibility:

♦ Achieving results through others

♦ Creating a encouraging environment for success

♦ Obedience to God

ACHIEVING RESULTS THROUGH OTHERS

The leader's primary responsibility is to achieve results through the actions of others. Three major elements of leadership required for positive results are: clarifying and reinforcing the mission; equipping the team; and celebrating victories.

All people do things for a reason. The reason may not make sense or be logical to someone else, but it makes perfect sense to the person doing it. How many times have we, as parents, asked our teenagers after they did something that did not make sense to us, "What were you thinking?" Most of the time, their action was logical and made sense to them at the time, but made absolutely no sense to the parent. Though they may have been confused at the time as to what they were supposed to do based on peer pressure or just not thinking – they did it for their reason.

The main reason employees do things that may make no sense to the leader is because they are confused about what is expected or why it is important. They perceive that one day the mission is one thing, the next day something else, the performance review reflects one thing, upper management says another thing, they heard the tone of your voice say something else, you reward yet another thing … get the picture? The leader's role is to provide clarity – crystal clear clarity – to the mission by making sure that all actions lead in the same direction and answer the question, "WHY are we doing this?"

People who do not understand why they should be doing something think they have a logical reason not to do it. It is natural for them to respond better when they understand why they are asked to do something. The "just do it" mentality does not motivate people to get the job done. No matter how often you talk about expectations, you will not accomplish your goals until you clearly define the "what" and "why" of your expectations. If you leave your team confused about your expectations, don't act confused when they don't do what you expect.

Another barrier to achieving results through others is that they are not equipped properly to do the job. They don't know how to do what you want them to do. Putting people in a position without training is putting people in a position to fail. Many leaders assume their followers know how to do their jobs when, in fact, they do not know and are afraid to ask.

Ecclesiastes 10:10 says this about training: *"If the ax is dull and its edge unsharpened, more strength is needed but skill will bring success."* Do not limit your success by limiting your training budget.

The third area of the leader's responsibility is to celebrate the victories! One basic leadership principle is what you reward, gets done. Some people will argue that wages are the reward, but the positive consequence most people are searching for is personal recognition from their leaders. "Tell me that you appreciate the work I do" is their cry.

Even with our best intentions, sometimes we reward failure and punish the people who are doing what needs to be done instead of celebrating victories.

Why would anyone be rewarded for failure? It happens all the time. People might work more slowly and be rewarded with overtime pay. People who complain about difficult tasks are given the easy tasks. People late to meetings are rewarded with a brief summary of what they missed while everyone else participated. Or, how many times have you heard people say, "Why does our company keep [him] around?" Watch what you are rewarding.

Also, watch what you are punishing. Many times the people who are working with us to accomplish our goals are punished for helping us achieve them. I can hear your thoughts. "That is ridiculous. Why would anyone do that?" See if any of these situations sound familiar:

- ◆ A person who does tough tasks well is "rewarded" with more, or all, of the tough tasks.

- ◆ A person delivering truthful but bad news is "rewarded" with verbal abuse.

- ◆ A person who suggests an improvement is "rewarded" with the extra load of the work to carry out his or her own suggestion.

- ◆ The best salesperson is "rewarded" with a disproportionate share of the quota.

These are just a few of the ways people are punished for doing what we want them to do. Watch what you're rewarding!

The bottom line is that the leader has to continually clarify the vision, equip the team with the tools to be successful, celebrate the victories and get out of the way.

Many times, I have witnessed the leader as the stumbling block. The environment you create will ultimately lead to the failure or success of your team. An environment of open communication, respect, feedback, recognition and continual improvement will result in increased loyalty, decreased turnover and increased profits. Be aware of what you're doing that might limit your team's success.

CREATING AN ENCOURAGING ENVIRONMENT FOR SUCCESS

One of the principle responsibilities of Christians is to encourage others. Encouragement is the act of inspiring others with renewed courage, spirit and hope. It does not matter how successful, positive, secure or mature a person may appear ... genuine encouragement never fails to help. In fact, all people need to be encouraged by people they respect.

The Bibles says in Hebrews, *"Let us hold fast the confession of our hope without wavering, for he who promised is faithful, and let us consider how to stimulate one another to love and good deeds, not forsaking our own assembling together, as is the habit of some but encouraging one another...."*

One of the greatest things we can do is encourage another by lifting them up and helping them. It is easy – and maybe natural – to discourage others. The world is full of discouragers. We have a Christian duty to encourage one another and we all can do it!

It doesn't require a budget or special skill; it only requires our encouraging words and actions.

Okay, I can hear you saying, "But my boss is not encouraging. In fact, he is discouraging – so how can I be a positive encourager?"

I know exactly what you mean. It is frustrating, but your role as a leader is to create a positive environment for your people and also have a positive relationship with your boss – no matter what. Managing your relationship with your boss involves applying the same principles you use when leading your subordinates. What you control is your attitude and your actions. You cannot change the boss's behavior but you can lead by example so that others might choose to change.

In *The Seven Habits of Highly Effective People,*[5] Stephen Covey wrote about the importance of understanding what you can influence:

Your circle of influence consists of things that you control. The more you focus energy on what you influence, the more you are able to influence. When you accept responsibility for all you control, you have done your job and, eventually, you will see positive changes happening outside your area of control!

OBEDIENCE TO GOD

As Christian leaders, we accept responsibility for our obedience to God. Regardless of the circumstance, we are responsible for others seeing Jesus in us and for living our commitment to Christ through our actions. This commitment is under our control. We should not be concerned about the reaction of others to our obedience to God.

SUMMARY

When you accept your leadership role, a change in responsibility comes along with the change in title. You always lead, and everything you do counts. You are responsible for everything you control including:

1. Achieving results through others

2. Creating an atmosphere of encouragement for your team, and

3. Your obedience to God.

Enjoy taking responsibility, and you will enjoy greater results in all areas of your life.

"One's philosophy is not best expressed in words; it's expressed in the choices one makes. In the long run we shape our lives and we shape ourselves. The process never ends until we die. And the choices we make are ultimately our responsibility."
– Eleanor Roosevelt

CHAPTER FOUR

COMMITMENT

Whoever wants to be great among you must be your servant.
And whoever wants to be greatest of all must be the slave of all.
– Mark 10:43-44 (LB)

THE PRINCIPLE OF COMMITMENT

Leadership results improve to the extent that the leader respects, recognizes, and develops his/her team.

L eading others does not require skill.

Look around – there are many people in leadership positions without vision, courage, integrity, optimism, or many of the other principles discussed in this book. They are leaders without leadership. Most of those leaders are leading people who are threatened by the loss of the job and feel they have no other choice.

A leader can pay people to follow, but who wants followers who are not **committed**?

More than 100 years ago, a missionary society wrote to David Livingstone as he explored Africa and asked, "Have you found a good road to where you are? If so, we want to know how to send other men to join you." Livingstone wrote back, "If you have men who will come only if they know there is a good road, I don't want them. I want men who will come if there is no road at all."

Committed teams understand the mission and commit to do what is necessary to accomplish the mission, whether there is a road or not. Developing this commitment requires a leader who recognizes, respects and rewards his followers. Committed followers are the result of a leader who follows the leadership principles illustrated in the Bible.

When Moses was called to lead his people out of Egypt, both God and Moses knew that Moses could not do it alone. Moses had a weakness – he was slow of speech – and God provided Aaron to cover that weakness. Moses could not have been as effective without Aaron, and Aaron certainly did not have the ability to lead by himself. Aaron was committed to do what was necessary to assist Moses in leading the people.

Moses also chose Joshua, a great strategist, who was totally committed to God and the mission. Joshua ultimately replaced Moses and played a key role in the exodus from Egypt. Joshua trained with Moses, his role model, until it was time for him to become the leader. He was prepared for his opportunity.

MORE EXAMPLES OF COMMITMENT

In 1921, history was made at New York City's Kane Summit Hospital. Veteran surgeon Dr. Evan O'Neill Kane performed an appendectomy using local anesthesia for the first time. Dr. Kane had been a crusader against the hazards of general anesthesia, contending that the use of local anesthesia was far safer. Not all of his colleagues believed his theory. They needed proof.

Dr. Kane searched for a volunteer to prove his theory, but many were squeamish. Finally, the surgeon found a candidate who was prepped and wheeled him into the surgical suite. Dr. Kane then took the scalpel and performed the surgery. During the procedure, the patient complained only of minor discomfort. He was then placed in a hospital ward and dismissed in two days. Thanks to the brave volunteer, Dr. Kane demonstrated that local anesthesia was not only a viable alternative to general anesthesia, it was preferred. Who was the courageous volunteer for Dr. Kane's experimental surgery? Dr. Kane, himself. A man so committed to his belief that he performed the appendectomy on himself. The doctor became a patient in order to convince the patients to trust the doctor.

This is the same kind of commitment Jesus used to develop committed followers. Through-out His ministry, He consistently demonstrated three leadership qualities that separated Him from other leaders at that time:

♦ Jesus was compassionate toward His followers – He loved them and provided direction for them. *"When He saw the crowds, He had compassion on them, because they were harassed and helpless, like sheep without a shepherd."*[1] He recognized a need and cared for all of them while providing them hope for the future.

♦ Jesus met their individual needs. He ministered to the suffering, the lame, the blind, the crippled and the hungry. He did what was necessary to meet their needs, and they were satisfied.[2]

♦ Jesus taught them in ways they could understand and relate to.[3] His message to His followers was clear.

Jesus also surrounded Himself with disciples, each with different skills and abilities. The disciples were ordinary men who, through Jesus' leadership, became extraordinary followers who led others to understand Jesus and contributed to the spreading of the Gospel.

LEVELS OF FOLLOWERSHIP
Successful leaders today develop a team of people who have different talents that complement each other's strengths. They also understand that people are motivated for different reasons. Regardless of who the leader is, there are three types of followers:

The first group includes those who follow because they have to – they simply feel they have no choice. They feel threatened if they do not follow. They may be threatened by the loss of their jobs, changing their standard of living, losing friends, upsetting their spouse, or something else important to them.

In most cases, these people are the most common and least effective. Once the threat goes away (their only reason for being on the team anyway) they quit following. Threats create temporary responses, so leaders must keep threatening these people to continue getting results. What a lousy way to lead and a miserable way to have to follow!

The second group contains people who follow because they choose to follow. They have an innate desire to accomplish a goal, regardless of who is leading. These people are content to do their jobs and focus primarily on their own activities without concern for the overall goal. Not great, but more effective than the first group.

The third group is the most effective: people who are committed to the leader and to the cause. These followers understand the mission, know the costs, and will do whatever is necessary to accomplish the mission. They are totally committed and will run through walls to make it happen!

While working at FedEx, I saw, firsthand, the impact of positive people working toward a common goal. When Fred Smith created FedEx, he was surrounded by a few committed people. Not many others believed his concept would work – it was a little too far "out of the box." Their question was, "Why would you deliver a package from San Francisco to Los Angeles through Memphis?"

His Yale professor gave him a "C" on the paper that he wrote explaining his idea. The investment community considered his concept illogical. Would you invest your money or career in such a radical concept?

Mark Twain once said, "The man with a new idea is a crank until the idea succeeds," and there were plenty of people calling Fred Smith a crank in the early '70s. But, Fred Smith understood his mission and invited some committed people to join him. And in April 1973, FedEx became a reality.

You can imagine the excitement on the first night of operation! Fourteen FedEx planes in fourteen cities made their first midnight trip to Memphis. The packages were sorted and then reloaded on planes that would take them to their destinations. The entire FedEx team was waiting to count the packages and celebrate their success.

One by one they unloaded the planes. When all the packages were counted, there were twelve packages on the fourteen planes. Two more planes than packages! That is not a good business model.

Can you imagine how discouraging the first night's results must have been?

Sure, everyone was disappointed. But Fred Smith had created a team of people who understood the long-term mission and were committed to pay the price to make it successful. In fact, when things were tough in the early days, several pilots paid for their planes' fuel with personal credit cards to keep them in the air. Those people were committed, and as they say, the rest of the story is history.

Tonight, FedEx will sort and deliver more than three million packages. Revenues will be over $40 billion in 2005. More than 300,000 employees are on the payroll, thanks to those first committed employees and the leadership of Fred Smith.

Your situation may not lead to a FedEx success story. However, wherever you are, you can leverage your success by increasing the number of committed people on your team and decreasing the number of people who are with you only because they have to be there.

BUILDING A COMMITTED TEAM

There are four keys to developing a committed team:

1. ***You must be committed, yourself.*** Before you can ask anyone to commit to your leadership, you have to make the decision to be a committed leader. There is no middle ground. Jesus spoke to the church in Laodicea about indifference: *"I know*

your deeds, that you are neither cold nor hot. I wish you were either one or the other! So because you are lukewarm — neither hot nor cold — I am about to spit you out of my mouth."[4] Everyone can understand Jesus' analogy. No one enjoys the disgusting taste of lukewarm water! The committed Christian cannot follow Jesus halfway, and the Christian leader must be committed to those he is leading.

Commitment requires action! Deciding to be committed and doing something about your commitment are entirely different. For instance, if three frogs were on a lily pad and one decided to jump, how many frogs would be left on the lily pad? If you said three, you are right! Deciding to jump and actually jumping are different actions. Jumping requires action. Deciding to jump is a step toward action but does not require commitment.

Leaders must do more than decide — they have to take action.

2. ***Surround yourself with people who have talent to do the job and a desire to do the job right.*** Picking the team is your most important function as a leader because your success rests, primarily, on the success of your team. Former basketball coach Nolan Richardson, enjoys sharing the wisdom of his grandmother and her impact on his life. "A great jockey can't win with a poor horse, but an average jockey can win with a good horse. Son, always get yourself a good horse." She knew the importance of surrounding yourself with talented people!

Hiring talented people with different backgrounds and experiences creates diversity as well as success. When Jesus was describing the body of Christ, He was teaching the value of diversity. *"God has combined the members of the body ... but that it's parts should have equal concern for each other. If one part suffers, every part suffers with it; if one part is honored, every part rejoices with it ... and in the church God has appointed ... apostles, prophets, teachers, workers of miracles, those having gifts of healing, those able to help others, administrators, and speakers."*[5] A successful team includes a variety of talents and experiences a leader can use to make each member more effective as part of a team than by themselves.

3. In addition to being committed and surrounding yourself with talented people, you must **dehire the people who are not carrying their load.** Is that the Christian thing to do? Absolutely. If you have given them an opportunity to succeed and their performance is hindering others, it is the best course of action for the employee, your work group and you. If you choose to keep people who are not right for the job, you are cheating them, yourself and everyone else on your team.

Most teams are composed of three performance groups. I call them super stars, middle stars, and falling stars.

The first is a group of outstanding performers: the "super stars." You know who they are, typically 10 to 20 percent of your team – maybe even 30 percent – who do everything you ask. You probably would like a larger percentage of super stars, but often they are promoted (up and out) to additional responsibilities ... which is the way it should be.

Your super stars earned their way into that category by being consistently outstanding performers. Don't overlook them! In some organizations, super stars become "the abused" as opposed to "the rewarded" because they have to take up the slack for those on the team who are not carrying their share of the load. That is not a good deal.

The second group – normally about half of your team – are "middle stars." They are not super stars, but they could be in the future. Their performance could also fall backward. They are your variable performers. Some days they exceed your expectations and on other days, they fall a bit short of what's expected.

As the largest group on your team, the middle stars are the backbone. Your ability to affect the performance of this group is critical any leader's success. One of the greatest influences on this group is how you treat the super star and falling star. They are watching you and making a decision on which to become based on your actions.

The last group is the falling stars. This group is usually quite small, but their impact can be quite large. These people consistently fail to carry their share of the load. In fact, not only are they not doing their own jobs, there's a good chance they're preventing the top performers from doing their jobs as well. This is a group that must be dealt with for you to achieve long-term success.

A person who is not right for the job and who creates a negative environment within the work group will destroy your team. It is your responsibility to eliminate the barriers to your team's performance, and if you refuse to address the problem of an incompetent employee, you may need to re-evaluate just who is incompetent.

The impact of keeping unproductive members on your team is illustrated by a golf experience of mine. I love golf and have discovered many leadership lessons from playing the game, which I shared in *Birdies, Pars & Bogeys: Leadership Lessons from the Links*. One of the most vivid lessons learned is the parallel of choosing the right equipment in golf and hiring the right employee at work.

For instance, I once bought a new golf club – a three wood – that was to be the answer to improve my game. It had the latest technology and looked great! The golf magazines gave this club the highest ratings. I was proud of my new club until I started hitting balls with it. I hit hundreds of balls on the driving range and on the course. The ball just would not go where I wanted it to go. You can imagine how frustrated I was.

Finally, after an investment of $299, hours of practice and many bad shots on the course, I had to make a decision – What was I going to do with this new club?

One of my alternatives was to leave the three wood in the bag and try to fool myself into thinking I had not made a mistake. The problem with the "ignore it" alternative was that I still needed a club to hit the distance of a three wood. The rules allow me to carry only 14 clubs, so keeping the club I could not hit would prevent me from getting another club that I would trust and could hit consistently. Ignoring the problem was not a good choice.

Another alternative was to keep using the new three wood. Even after hundreds of bad hits, my pride was telling me that I could work it out. I tried one more round and was again rewarded with slices, hooks, rough, trees, sand and out-of-bounds shots. Hitting this club was driving me crazy, hurting my game, killing my confidence, and affecting my attitude. Continuing to use the club was not the answer to my problem.

The alternative I chose was to accept the fact that this club was not right for me. Even though it was highly recommended and a great club for other golfers, it was not the right club for my game. I chose to accept my financial loss, and loss of pride, and sell it to someone more suited for the club. My friend who bought it from me (for $75) became a better golfer with the same club that was hurting my attitude, patience and score.

Now I have a new three wood that I hit well and feel confident hitting. The problem was not my swing or my club. The problem was that my swing was not right for that particular club. Once I accepted the fact that I had done everything I could with the expensive, high-tech, good-looking club that did not work for me, I was able to improve my game.

The same lesson applies to your work. People who are not the best fit for your position will be an exact fit for someone else's position. The faster you act after making a decision to dehire, the better for you, your employee and your work group.

The single greatest demotivator of a team is to have members who are not carrying their load. It takes courage to let people go. Your emotions are involved, the employee's emotions and short-term livelihood are involved, and it is a tough conversation to have. If you have provided someone every opportunity for success, yet his performance fails to meet expectations, summon your courage and allow him to go where he can be successful. It is not a personal mistake of yours, nor is it a mistake of the employee – the job is just not right for him.

The worst thing you can do is to have someone who has already quit (mentally) still on the team.

Here's the good news. In a survey by Clayton Sherman Leadership House, conducted only one year after employees were discharged, 80 percent of former employees reported their separation to be "the best thing that ever happened to me." As unbelievable as that may sound, many dehires force people to move from a job that isn't right for them to something more aligned with their talents and interests. With few exceptions, it's also the best thing for the remainder of the team ... and the leader.

4. The fourth requirement to develop a committed team is for you to **become a servant leader**. Jesus' blueprint included caring for followers, addressing their individual needs and teaching them in ways they understand. Your role is to listen to their ideas, always treat them with respect even when their ways differ from yours, and provide direction for their success.

Caring for your followers involves *serving* them rather than *using* them. Servant leaders know the value of their followers and are givers, not takers. Remember, you need your team at least as much as they need you.

Jesus is our example of servant leadership. He served others to the extent that He gave His life away. Jesus washed the feet of His disciples and told them *"no master is greater than his servant."*[6] He was a servant to His followers.

Caring for your team also involves recognizing and motivating them to make contributions.

In the CornerStone seminars, we ask participants to rank sequentially what motivates them. Out of thousands of people, more than 80 percent said recognition of accomplishment is the number one motivator. Not money, not benefits, not time off – just recognize me for what I do.

Here are the top five values of the employees surveyed:

1. Show appreciation for the job I do.

2. Allow me to be involved. Don't just tell me what to do.

3. When I have a problem, help me work through it.

4. Pay me fairly.

5. Provide me with safe working conditions.

Isn't it interesting that the interpersonal side of leadership – being appreciated, asked for input and supported by a person who cares – was more important than money, promotion and growth? Employees' sense of worth is more valuable than their paycheck.

SUMMARY

Your success depends on developing a committed team and serving them. There is no scarcity of feet to wash. Many times the stumbling block to our team's commitment is our own lack of willingness to do what we ask others to do.

Several years ago, research at North Carolina's Center for Creative Leadership identified the chief causes of executive failure in organizations. At the very top of their list were arrogance and insensitivity to other people. The next factor was betrayal of trust.

Jesus warned us to control our egos, not to be arrogant, and to be sensitive to our followers. *"For everyone who exalts himself will be humbled, and he who humbles himself will be exalted."*[7] Successful leadership requires serving your followers.

Make the decision today to be committed. Surround yourself with the very best people, dehire the people not contributing and create an environment that supports your team's commitment.

The ultimate test of leadership is what happens when the leader is not around. ***There cannot be successful leadership without dedicated followership, and there cannot be dedicated followers without committed leaders.***

THE CHRISTIAN LEADER'S COMMITMENT

It would not be right to leave a chapter dedicated to commitment without speaking about our commitment to Christ. The direction we have been provided is clear: *"Love the Lord your God with **all** your heart and with **all** your soul and with **all** your mind and with **all** your strength."*[8]

That is total commitment – not lukewarm, not part-time, not halfway – total commitment to Christ. When we become totally committed, we can trust God that everything else will take care of itself.

Eugene Habecker suggested six evidences of intense commitment to Christ in his book *"Leading With a Follower's Heart."*[9] Here are his questions to check our commitment:

1. Do I live contrary to the ways of the world? *"Do not love the world or anything in the world. If anyone loves the world, the love of the Father is not in him."*[10]

2. Am I prepared to experience and/or suffer persecution? *"In fact, everyone who wants to live a godly life in Christ Jesus will be persecuted."*[11]

3. Do I place little value on material things? *"For where your treasure is, there your heart will be also."*[12]

4. Will I gladly and willingly surrender my personal rights? Christ is our example: *"Not my will, but yours be done."*[13]

5. Am I prepared to be involved in the lives of others? *"Carry each other's burdens, and in this way you will fulfill the law of Christ."*[14]

6. I am not ashamed of Christ and His words. *"If anyone is ashamed of me and my words in this adulterous and sinful generation, the Son of Man will be ashamed of him when he comes in his Father's glory with the holy angels."*[15]

When we can unequivocally answer yes to each of these questions, we will exhibit the total commitment Christ asks from us.

CHAPTER FIVE

VISION

Where there is no vision, the people perish.
– Proverbs 29:18 (KJV)

THE PRINCIPLE OF VISION

**Leadership results improve when leaders communicate
a crystal clear vision and a convincing reason
to accomplish the vision.**

Three people were working side by side on a construction job. When they were asked, "What is your job?" the first person replied, "My job is to do what I am told for eight hours so I can get a check." The second person said, "My job is to crush rocks." The third person replied, "My job is to help build a cathedral."

Which of those three people do you think would be the most productive and have the greater self-esteem?

No doubt the third person, who understood his role was far greater than just crushing rocks. He understood the vision and had a sense of purpose. His leader had focused on the result and communicated the vision in a way that the worker was able to concentrate on the cathedral while accomplishing the task at hand – crushing rocks.

Effective leaders have the ability to look where most people cannot see. They are able to see beyond the obvious and focus on something greater than the current situation. They have is a clear understanding of what could be and the ability to communicate the vision well enough so that others will want to make the choice to follow.

DREAMS CAN BECOME A LIFELONG VISION

One night as the family was ending its evening, young Jimmy went upstairs to bed without being told. When his parents headed for their bedroom, his mother looked in to check on their young son – and there he was, gazing out of his window looking up at the moon.

"What are you doing son?" his mother asked, as she carried him to his bed and pulled up the covers.

"One day, Mommy, I'm going to walk on the moon," the youngster replied.

Thirty-two years later, when James Irwin stepped onto the lunar surface, he achieved that vision as he joined an elite group of the human race who left their footprints on the moon.

James Irwin's dream became his lifelong vision!

BIBLICAL EXAMPLES OF VISION

Throughout the Old Testament, God provided direction and then presented a vision of the result of that direction. God told Abram,

"Leave your country and I will make you into a great nation, bless you, make your name great, and all people will be blessed through you."[1] What a vision! That was certainly something greater than Abram's current situation.

God gave Moses a clear vision to *"bring my people, the Israelites, out of Egypt."*[2] Although Moses did not understand all the methods needed to make that happen or the challenges he would face, his mission was clear.

Nehemiah's vision was clear, *"Let us rebuild the walls of Jerusalem, and we will no longer be in disgrace."*[3]

In the New Testament, Jesus spoke often of our spiritual vision. *"The eye is the lamp of the body. If your eyes are good, your whole body will be full of light. But if your eyes are bad, your whole body will be full of darkness. If then the light within you is darkness, how great is that darkness!"*[4] Jesus was speaking of our capacity to know what God wants from us and to keep our eyes focused on the goal.

When Jesus chose his disciples, His vision was clear: *"I will make you fishers of men."* From fishers of fish to fishers of men – they understood, for *"at once they left their nets and followed Him."*[5] They saw something greater than their current situation.

Jesus also had a crystal clear vision for His ministry, which He communicated in the synagogue in Nazareth: *"The spirit of the Lord is on me, because he has anointed me to preach good news to the poor. He has sent me to proclaim freedom for the prisoners and recovery of sight for the blind, to release the oppressed, to proclaim the year of the Lord's favor."*[6] He knew what He was to accomplish.

The disciples continually needed the vision reinforced ... because every time they were afraid, anxious or confused, they lost the vision. Sounds familiar doesn't it? Our team is exactly the same – fear, anxiety and confusion often blurs their vision. Good decisions are difficult to make under the stress of fear, anxiety, or confusion! *The leader's purpose is to calm the unrest, develop trust to eliminate anxiety, and give clear direction to eliminate confusion.*

A leader must deliver a vision that vividly explains how each person makes a difference, and one in which his team can see a worthwhile result. It must be a vision that generates energy, enthusiasm and commitment among the people. A vision that clearly provides a consistency of purpose. One so focused that, as Peter Drucker says, you become "A monomaniac with a mission."

If your team is concerned only with survival and have no sense of purpose you will never achieve long-term, lasting results.

THE "I HAVE A DREAM" VISION

Martin Luther King was able to express his vision in a vivid, clear, moving way that generated energy, enthusiasm and commitment from his followers. Read the vision he communicated in his famous "I Have A Dream" speech:

> *I say to you today, my friends, that in spite of the difficulties and frustration of the moment I still have a dream ... I have a dream that one day in the red hills of Georgia the sons of former slaves and the sons of former slave owners will be able to sit down together at the table of brotherhood. I have a dream that one day even the state of Mississippi, a desert state sweltering with the heat of injustice and oppression, will be transformed into an oasis of freedom and justice. I have a dream that my four little children will one day live in a*

nation where they will not be judged by the color of their skin but by the content of their character. I have a dream … of that day when all of God's children, black men and white men, Jews and Gentiles, Protestants and Catholics, will be able to join hands and sing in the words of the old Negro spiritual, "Free at last! Free at last! Thank God almighty, we are free at last!"[7]

Martin Luther King's vision was clear, easily understood, and focused on looking forward to something far greater than his current situation.

A MATTER OF FOCUS

Focus is defined as "directing energy toward a particular point or purpose." Certainly, there are many external factors that can make it difficult for teams to stay focused on what's important. Business is a very complex and multi-faceted arena. And the more complicated things are, the easier it is to lose focus.

Even in the early part of the 20th century, Henry Ford believed a weakness of all human beings was trying to do too many things at once. "That scatters effort and destroys direction," he said. "Every now and then I wake up in the morning with a dozen things I want to do. I know I can't do them all at once.' When asked what he did about that, Ford replied, "I go out and trot around the house. While I'm running off the excess energy that wants to do too much, my mind clears and I see what can be done and should be done first."

But, that's where good leadership comes in … that's where YOU come in. All too often those in the lead become the sources of complexity and instability rather than solutions.

Creating and maintaining a laser-sharp focus for the team is at the very heart of leadership. And, be assured, it's much easier said than done.

Today's fast-paced environment demands flexible organizations – ones that are ready to adapt to changing market conditions and technical innovations. But, constant changes and the distractions that accompany them can cause us to blur our focus, overcommit and lock into a knee-jerk response mode ... not a good place for leaders, or their followers, to be.

When leaders fail to maintain their focus, the team will aimlessly wander in search of direction and clarity. Employees don't know where to aim ... where to direct their energy and attention.

This confusion and complexity creates dissatisfaction and frustration. If people don't understand how their role ties to the big picture, it's difficult to keep everyone pulling together in the same direction.

Under these out-of-focus conditions, if the team happens to hit a target and achieve its goal (and that's a BIG "IF"), it will be because of luck rather than leadership. The problem with luck is that it's fleeting and unpredictable ... and eventually runs out.

CREATING THE VISION
How do you create a vision?

The *first* step begins with you – you have to be totally committed to the task. If you are serious about wanting to lead people, you must first be serious about leading yourself.

Martin Luther King demonstrated his commitment through his activism – there was no question about his commitment. He was committed enough to lead unpopular demonstrations, committed enough to go to jail. He had a vision … and he never lost sight of that dream.

The less commitment you have, the more blurred your vision becomes. You cannot fake commitment. People see through an uncommitted leader like a crystal glass. If you are not committed, don't lead … don't even think about it.

Second, dream of the way things should be – not as they are. Ask yourself, "What is possible?" A vivid vision of the result keeps everyone motivated. Not many people really understood Fred Smith's vision for FedEx or Martin Luther King's vision for equal rights. But for these great leaders the vision was vividly clear, and they never missed an opportunity to share their visions with their followers.

Third, put your vision in writing. Putting things on paper creates clarity. A vision in writing becomes a mission, and once your mission is clear, you have accomplished one of the most difficult tasks of leadership.

Ultimately, your team's ownership of the vision determines its success. Don't let people guess about where you, and where they, are headed. Chances are, they will guess wrong. Communicate often and consistently to all levels of the organization.

Your ability to get others to see the vision and follow your direction depends upon your team believing in you long before they invest in the vision. Acceptance of your vision occurs long after their acceptance of you.

How People Respond
Even though you clearly communicate the vision, have earned

trust, and have commitment to the goal, not all people will respond in the same manner.[8]

♦ *Some will never be able to see your vision.* Their cry, "Show me, show me and then show me." They just can't grasp the result. They can still be good followers, but you will have to lead them with explicit directions to get them to go where you want them to go. They are very high maintenance, will drain you of your energy and will keep you from spending time with your other employees.

♦ *Some will see the vision but just do not care.* This group is dangerous. Their cry is, "So what?" They see what you are trying to accomplish but do not have the desire to pay the price to reach it. This group is the least productive and can influence others to be less productive. You can train skills – you can't train desire.

If you choose to keep these employees on your team, you have to be totally involved with them to help them embrace the vision. If you have many people on your team in this category, your chance for success is not good and your chances of enjoying your job are even worse. These people will keep you awake at night.

• *Some will see the vision and go after it.* Their battle cry is, "Yes, let's do it!" You empower them to accomplish the vision. Then let them go. They are great followers. They respond to positive reinforcement and positive leadership. Keep showing them the vision and they will keep going after it. These followers will keep you motivated, and you will enjoy witnessing their accomplishments.

- *Some will see the vision and lead others toward it.* Their cry is, "Let's do it, and I will help lead others to go with us!" You lead this important group with encouragement, then get out of their way and let them lead. They are your most valuable asset.

Your chances for success increase in proportion to the percentage of followers you have in this group. They will challenge you to continue to improve the vision and keep it refreshed. Nurture, mentor and support these people!

If your leadership only influences others to follow, your results are limited by what you can personally do. If you influence others to lead, then your results are unlimited.

THE TOUGH PART

Developing the vision is actually the easy part.

The tough part? Maintaining your focus despite any challenges or obstacles along the way. As a leader, your commitment must be to identify and diligently focus on your vision.

The truth is, it's usually leaders – not followers – responsible for frequent changes in team direction and focus. But beware! If your focus is always changing, expect nothing but frustrated employees. If you stay focused, you increase the likelihood that your team will meet its goals.

Maintaining a laser-sharp focus on accomplishing goals is neither natural nor easy. Without question, you will face distractions that pull you away from your vision. That's okay as long as you quickly get back on track. Your job is to continually hone your focus, communicate the vision and keep the team on target and, by doing so, ensure your team's success – and yours as well.

SUMMARY

People follow leaders who know where they are going. Only a fool would board a plane without knowing its destination. You should not expect people to follow without you communicating where you are going.

Excellent leadership vision does not necessarily guarantee excellent results, yet leadership without vision guarantees failure. Many leaders have a great vision but are not successful, because they are unable to communicate the vision in a way their team can understand. If you effectively communicate the vision, earn your team's trust and remove obstacles, your followers will commit to the vision and will be willing to pay the price to make the vision a reality.

Vision is the gift of seeing clearly what may be.
Vision expands our horizons.
The more we see, the more we can achieve;
the grander our vision, the more glorious our accomplishment.
The courage to follow our dreams is the first step toward destiny.
—Wynn Davis

PART TWO

THE SYNERGY PRINCIPLES

COMMUNICATION ♦ OVERCOMING ADVERSITY
OPTIMISM ♦ POSITIVE CHANGE

The leader who fosters a positive, winning atmosphere –
regardless of the situation –
can achieve results beyond their imagination.

CHAPTER SIX

COMMUNICATION

Do not let unwholesome talk come out of your mouths, but only what is helpful
for building others up according to their areas, that it may benefit those who listen.
— Ephesians 4:29

THE PRINCIPLE OF COMMUNICATION

Results improve when followers understand their roles and
are rewarded for their accomplishments by their leaders.

If you have seen the classic clip of Abbott and Costello's "Who's on First?" routine, you will probably remember this hilarious exchange between the two men. A baseball manager (Abbott) was telling Costello the names of his players: "Who" was on first, "What" was on second, "I Don't Know" was on third, "Why" was in left field, "Because" was in center, "Tomorrow" was the pitcher, and "I Don't Give A Darn" was the shortstop. The scene went like this:

Costello: So you're the manager. You know, I would like to know some of the guys' names so when I meet them at the ballpark, I'll be able to say hello.

Abbott: Sure, I will introduce you to the boys. They give them funny names, though, Lou.

Costello: I know. They give them all funny names.

Abbott: Let's see. Who is on first, What's on second, and I Don't Know is on third.

Costello: (Interrupts) You the manager?

Abbott: Yes.

Costello: You know the guys' names?

Abbott: I should.

Costello: Then tell me the guys' names.

Abbott: I said, "Who is on first, What's on second, I Don't Know is on third."

Costello: (Interrupts) You the manager?

Abbott: Yes.

Costello: You know the guys' names?

Abbott: I'm telling you their names.

Costello: Then go ahead and tell me.

Abbott: Who's on first.

Costello: Who?

Abbott: The guy on first.

Costello: Who?

Abbott: The guy on first. Who is on first.

Costello: What are you asking me for? I am asking who is on first?

Abbott: I'm telling you. Who is on first.

Costello: You ain't telling me anything. I am asking who is on first.

Abbott: That's right.

Costello: Then go ahead and tell me.

Abbott: Who.

Costello: The guy on first base.

Abbott: That's his name.

Costello: Then go ahead and tell me.

Abbott: That's the man's name.

Costello: That's whose name?

Abbott: Who is on first.

Costello: What you are asking me for? I am asking you who is on first.

Abbott: That's right. Who is on first.

And on and on it went as Abbott and Costello "communicated" in furious agreement for eight more of the greatest comedy minutes in the history of television.

Have you ever felt you were in a "Who's on First?" conversation where everyone was talking but no one was understanding … or listening?

Since Adam whispered his first words to Eve, people have been communicating. Billions of words are spoken every day. But, communication isn't just about talking. It's about connecting with one of the deepest needs of all people … to be understood.

Family counselors will confirm that connected communication is the missing ingredient in broken homes. Schoolteachers will verify that communication skills are essential to social acceptance even in preschool. Your ability to communicate effectively is one of the requirements of effective leadership in all areas of your life.

In business, the issue most often voiced is, "Our organization does not communicate."

Employees become frustrated, feeling they're always "out of the loop" and no one really cares. Leadership becomes frustrated, saying "All we do is communicate – they just do not listen."

Both sides could be right.

Research shows the average person wastes over five hours per week – over seven weeks a year – due to unclear communication! What are they missing?

Effective communication is a two-way exchange of ideas, methods, or reasoning that is understood – or connected – by both parties. All people have communication needs that must be addressed by their leaders. No matter how much you voice mail, e-mail, memo or speak, if you are not clearly connecting, you're not addressing your team's needs.

Most leaders spend so much time and effort communicating, it's hard for them to believe it could be a major problem. The paradox is that while followers are frustrated by a lack of communication, most leaders feel they are outstanding communicators. In one study, researchers asked a group of managers to evaluate their personal communication skills. The study discovered that 90 percent of leaders rate their communication skills in the top 10 percent of all leaders. Obviously, 80 percent of the leaders think they are better communicators then they actually are.

Actually, communication may not be the problem, and communicating more may not be the solution. In most cases, people do not need more information. Most of the information they receive doesn't get read; that which gets read is frequently not understood; and that which is understood is usually not remembered. So, communicating more will probably not help ... connecting more will.

DISCONNECTED COMMUNICATION

When a young FBI employee was put in charge of the FBI's supply department, he decided to reduce the size of the office's memo paper to save money and, in doing so, to impress his boss – J. Edgar Hoover.

When one of the new memo sheets ended up on Hoover's desk, the director took one look and determined he didn't like the smaller size of the margins and scrawled across the memo, "Watch the borders!"

For the next six weeks, it was extremely difficult to enter the United States from Mexico or Canada. Why? The FBI was watching the borders.

Ultimately, the real problem occurs when the communication being delivered is not the same as, or connected with, the message being received. In other words, the communication is often filled with so much static that the message is not understood, supported or accepted by employees.

Like Hoover's message about wanting memo paper with wider borders, the "static" preventing his staff from understanding that communication could be ambiguity, confusion, inconsistency, conflict, fear or distrust.

The ability to communicate effectively by connecting with people of different educational levels, backgrounds and maturity is essential to a great leader. *Effective communication is the most important way to develop trust and commitment.* People will not follow leaders without clearly understanding where they are going and why.

BIBLICAL EXAMPLES OF HOW TO COMMUNICATE

The Bible illustrates communications that were specific to the abilities of the followers to understand, comprehend, and act upon. Jesus chose to communicate through parables, often multiple parables with the same meaning. He knew that people could **relate to the experiences of other people**.

Through a fire in a bush, God communicated with Moses about becoming the leader of his people.[1] When Moses saw the bush burning without being consumed, he decided to investigate. Imagine being in the wilderness and seeing a bush burn, but never burn out. In this instance, the power of the Lord's communication was **using the unexpected** to get the attention of Moses.

Paul was a passionate communicator. Before his conversion, he was passionate in his persecution of Christians. After his conversion experience, Paul communicated the good news of Jesus with the same **sincerity and passion**. He was a great communicator because of his passion for what he was communicating. You could read Paul like a book, because he could never hide his passion and his commitment. He is my favorite writer in the Bible.

Jesus was a consistent, faithful communicator to God. He made communication a priority and acted upon the direction given. He was a **great listener**, a requirement for effective leadership.

Jesus also communicated by **touching people**. He went where the people were in order to touch them, be with them, provide direction and be empathetic to their needs. He communicated to them where they were comfortable, on their level – whether peasant or king – and he treated them as individuals.

Barnabas communicated through **encouragement**. He encouraged Paul through Paul's early days as a Christian. He risked his life supporting Paul when others were skeptical of Paul's conversion. By encouraging Paul and Mark, Barnabas had a direct and positive influence on the early Christian movement.

WHAT TO CONNECT

The greatest single impact on connected communication is trust. People will go out of their way to avoid communicating with those they do not trust. Your first responsibility in communication is to earn the other person's trust and respect. Without trust, you are wasting each other's time.

One obvious group requiring effective communication is the people you are leading. Each person on the team is motivated differently, creating unique demands upon the leader. The better you know your people, the more trust you will develop; and the better you connect, the more effective your leadership.

Regardless of individual differences, people have six basic connection requirements that the leader must address. Notice how Jesus met each of these needs with His followers.

1. ***Everyone Must Know What Is Expected of Them.*** You would think that all employees would know their purpose at work; however, ambiguity about roles in the workplace is the major

source of stress for employees. The following thoughts are typical in most companies:

We provide them job descriptions and expectations. I just do not understand why they are not doing what they are supposed to be doing.

—The Leader

I just don't know what they want.

—The Follower

How frustrating for both parties. Leaders cannot understand why they won't do what they should be doing, and followers don't understand why leaders are not clear in what they want. They are frustrated over the same issue ... their communication is not connected! What is required can be answered with job descriptions and job expectations, yet the real answer is communicated through your consistent message about your people's importance and purpose. The effective leader explains things personally and often. If someone is wondering what is required of him, the chances of his doing what you want are not very good. Make sure every person knows exactly what you want. Be consistent, communicate often and check for understanding. **No matter how often you talk about what you expect, you will not accomplish your goals unless your expectations are connected with your team's perceptions of your expectations.**

Jesus was clear about what was required of His followers. His followers had to make a decision to resign from their lives of independence and submit to authority. *"If anyone would come after me, he must deny himself and take up his cross daily and follow me. For whoever wants to save his life will lose it, but whoever loses his life will save it.*"[2] The expectations were clear, along with the reason it was important.

2. *People Must Understand How Their Leaders Think They Are Doing.* Regardless of the maturity of your team, every person has to know how they are doing. The second major source of stress, after ambiguity of roles, occurs when the person is unsure of how he is doing from the perspective of the leader. Employees can feel in control only of circumstances they understand and only when they know whether they are meeting expectations. Everyone needs encouragement. People are sensitive and desire to do a good job. It is human nature for people to want to know whether they are performing adequately or to be told what they can do to improve. It is the responsibility of the leader to **catch people doing things right and reinforce that behavior or let them know what they need to change to improve.**

The leadership style of Jesus was one of positive recognition and encouragement. God Himself praised Jesus at His baptism. *"And a voice came from heaven 'You are my Son whom I love; with you I am well pleased.'"*[3] The teachings of Jesus included servanthood, treating others with respect, and hope for the future. In the parable of the king's ten servants, Jesus used the example of the master praising the servant: *"Well done, my good servant."*[4] Positive feedback is a requirement for continued positive behavior.

If you are like most, you are pretty confident that you do a great job providing feedback. However, studies show that there is a significant difference in the perception of leaders and their team as to how often positive feedback is given.

In an extensive survey, managers were asked to respond to this statement: "I let my subordinates know when they are doing a good job." The subordinates responded to a similar statement: "My supervisor lets me know when I'm doing a good job." Same question, different perspective. A scale of 1 to 5 was used, where 1 = never and 5 = always.

The managers rated themselves a 4.3. The employees rated their managers a 2.3! A huge gap in perception![5] According to this study, for every positive recognition the leader receives only one half credit. Don't allow yourself to be fooled into thinking you recognize positive behavior too often. Do it twice as much as you think you should, and you will have a good chance of meeting people's needs.

Who was right or wrong in this survey is not the issue. The **perception** of the subordinates is what counts. Give positive feedback often!

3. *People Must Know Whether Anyone Cares.* Whether you consciously answer it or not, the question "Does anyone around here really care?" is always answered. Compassion and caring for your people, their sacrifices, and their contributions are communicated in the way you answer their question. The most effective way to show your team you care is to invest your time with your people. The more you invest, the greater your return. But, your investment must reflect what is important to your followers.

It is often not the mountain ahead, but the grain of sand in the shoe, that keeps you from reaching your goals. Many times the "grain of sand" is the lack of attention from the person who is supposed to be leading them. Some leaders are so focused on the "big things" that they forget to take care of the basic need of taking time to show their team they sincerely care about them. Showing you care does not require money or much time ... it only requires your focus and attention.

Jesus answered the question "Does anyone care?" with His leadership actions. He was an unselfish, compassionate teacher who prepared His followers for additional responsibilities. Even with those actions showing He cared, He was still asked the question, "Don't you care?" at least twice in his ministry. The disciples, who had seen His miracles in person, questioned Him when they were afraid and in perceived danger. When they were in their boat during a storm, they woke Jesus with the question, *"Teacher, don't you care?"*[6] When Martha was frustrated because she perceived that she was having to do her sister's work, she asked *"Lord, don't you care?"*[7] If Jesus had to answer this question, think how much more often we have to answer the same question for our followers. When is the last time your team saw you performing miracles?

"Don't you care?" has to be answered for your team when there is change or when they are afraid, uncertain or feel they are carrying too much of the load. You answer their question with your communication, actions and compassion.

4. ***Everyone Needs to Know How the Team Is Doing.*** People want to be a part of a winning team and know that their contributions are worthwhile. Establishing work unit goals, team expectations, and feedback on the team's progress is essential to effective leadership. The more emphasis you can have on teamwork, the greater the accountability your team

members will feel toward each other. Keep your team informed about whether they are winning or, if they are not winning, what they need to do to become winners.

Jesus was a team player. He believed in keeping peace on the team and having the team focused on the ultimate goal. When two of His team members, James and John, asked for preferential treatment and the remaining ten disciples became upset, Jesus called them together to settle them down and refocus their mission.[8] He reinforced the worthiness of their contributions and taught them that to be team players they were to serve, not be served.

5. *People Need to Know Where They Fit in the Big Picture.*
What are the company's goals, and what contribution does our team make toward its success? What is our impact on the total plan? Everyone needs to know their importance to the achievement of the overall goal.

Paul, on the road to Damascus, received clear direction on where he fit in God's plan and the result he was to expect. *"Now get up and stand on your feet. I have appeared to you to appoint you as a servant and as a witness of what you have seen and what I will show you ... I am sending you to them to open their eyes and turn them from darkness to light, and from the power of Satan to God, so that they may receive forgiveness of sins and a place among those who are sanctified by faith in me."*[9]

Jesus let His disciples know exactly where they fit in the Master's plan and what roles they were to accept. He told them of the trials they would face, the price of following Him, and the false signs that would be before them. He told them everything in advance so that they would know where they fit in and would be prepared for their responsibilities.[10]

6. ***People Need to Know How They Can Help.*** What can we do to make a positive difference? What can we do to make our organization better? Most people want to be a part of making a positive difference in the lives of others, and they need to know what they can do to make the difference.

When Jesus stated the great commission, He was clear in His instruction about what we are to do to help: *"Go and make disciples of all nations, baptizing them in the name of the Father, and of the Son and of the Holy Spirit, and teaching them to obey everything I have commanded you. And surely I am with you always to the very end of the age."*[11]

The responsibility of the leader is to address each of these six communication needs. If any of the needs are not being met, it is like rolling a wheel with a section missing. You may arrive at your destination, but it will not be a smooth trip and will take you a lot longer to get there. Be sensitive to each of these needs and create an ongoing plan to address each requirement.

KEEP THE MAIN THING THE MAIN THING

The responsibilities of leadership can be overwhelming at times. So many things come from different directions, making it difficult to separate the important from the trivial. One of the principle responsibilities of the leader is to keep the main thing the main thing – the one overriding point or purpose toward which all energy and attentions should be directed at that moment.

Jesus was a master at keeping the main thing the main thing. When Martha was so upset at Mary and questioned whether Jesus really cared, Jesus reminded her of what was important. *"Martha, Martha, you are worried and upset about many things, but only one thing is needed. Mary has chosen what is better and it will not be taken away from her."*[12] Jesus knew what was trivial and what was important, and he had Martha adjust her focus to the one thing that was important.

There are a few main things that will ultimately determine your success. If the energy and direction of your people are being used on anything other than those vital functions, energy is being wasted. Your responsibility is to eliminate all of the non-essentials and to keep your team focused on the few main things.

Peter Drucker said that everyone should always know the answer to these two questions: "What is our business?" and "How is business?" Your value as the leader is to provide clarity of purpose and consistently reward the accomplishment of the important few activities – the main things – which make the big difference.

One of my favorite classic movies is *City Slickers*. As a typical baby boomer, I can relate to many scenes in the movie. My favorite character was Curly, a hard, crusty old man full of wisdom. His best advice to Mitch, who was experiencing mid-life questions, was in this scene:

Curly: You all come out here about the same age. Same problems. Spend fifty weeks a year getting knots in your rope – then you think two weeks up here will untie them for you. None of you get it. Do you know what the secret of life is?

Mitch: No, what?

Curly: This. (Holds up his index finger.)

Mitch: Your finger?

Curly: One thing. Just one thing. You stick to that and everything else don't mean [anything].

Mitch: That's great, but what's the one thing?

Curly: That's what you've got to figure out.

Curly's "secret" is a personal relationship with Jesus Christ, but the same principle can be applied to your work group. Figure out what are your main things, spend your time and energy working on the main things and be the very best doing the main things.

MAKE LISTENING A PRIORITY

Take the time to listen attentively to your followers. Alexander Pope once observed, "Some people never learn anything because they understand everything too soon." Two of the greatest obstacles hindering improvement in productivity are the leaders' egos and their inability or desire to listen. One of the deepest needs of all people is to be listened to and understood. A person who is genuinely interested in what others have to say will state his opinion only after listening to everyone else's opinion. Listening is the way you show how much you value other people and what they are saying, and is also the way to build trust.

Listening effectively is not easy. It requires three things that not many leaders have an abundance of: time, patience and total concentration. As a leader, involved listening is an investment in your people. The better you listen, comprehend and act upon recommendations, the more trust you earn. If you listen to hear only what you want to hear, you lose trust. Don't just sit there! Listen attentively, don't interrupt, wait a few seconds before replying, ask questions and demonstrate you care by the attention you give. The best listeners make better decisions and become the best leaders.

PERSONAL CONTACT AND COMMUNICATION

In the CornerStone seminars, we ask the participants to list the
leadership characteristics of the most outstanding leader they know.
A consistent, number one characteristic is that the leader cares for
them personally. Successful leaders care for their people and
empathize with their needs. Just as in the time of Jesus, followers
have a need for personal contact and communication on their turf.
Jesus talked with people on all economic and social levels – the
rich, poor, royal, hermits, lawyers, criminals, children and adults. He
met them where they were comfortable and addressed their needs.
Many times He taught them while he was walking and/or eating,
because the listeners were relaxed.

Today, being face-to-face with your followers and meeting with them
on their turf requires dedicated effort. Technology has been a great
productivity enhancement in dealing with the technical side of
management, but it has been a detriment to maintaining personal
contact with your people. The explosion of e-mail and voice mail has
shackled many leaders to their offices, their computers or their phones.

When we're not communicating face-to-face, there's always room
for misunderstanding.

As the story goes, a woman of much dignity and decorum was
planning a two-week vacation in Florida and emailed the RV park
where she and her husband would be staying, asking for information.
One of her questions concerned the proximity of the toilet facilities
to the parking place they had been assigned, but being hesitant to
use the words "toilet facilities" in her letter she decided, instead, to
delicately use the initials "B.C." for bathroom-commode."

The park's owner, upon reading her email, was puzzled about the "B.C." reference but after conferring with his wife, decided the writer had meant "Baptist Church." The following was his response:

"The 'B.C.' is located nine miles north of the camp site but is capable of seating 250 people at one time. It is quite a distance away if you are in the habit of going regularly, but no doubt you will be pleased to know that a great number of people take their lunches along and make a day of it, arriving early and staying late. The last time my wife and I went was six years ago, and it was so crowded we had to stand up the whole time we were there. When you come down to the campground, perhaps I could go with you the first time you go ... sit with you ... and introduce you to all the other folks. This is really a very friendly community."

In this day and age of wireless technology, pagers, cell phones and walkie-talkies, it is sometimes a tremendous effort for leaders to make personal contact with their followers, just as Jesus made it a priority to lead by being there with the people he loved, the people he cared about.

Every employee, no matter how long they've worked for you or how talented they are, needs to know they are okay, and nothing replaces your personal communication of that message. A handshake, a pat on the back or a smile to say "thank you" has a far greater impact than any message on a computer screen.

It may seem strange, but the more you use technology in your communications the more you will need to have face-to-face communication with your followers. Don't allow your online communications to replace that personal touch in your communications. Electronics never develop trust.

COMMUNICATION WITH YOUR BOSS

Whether your boss is great or your relationship is strained, it is your responsibility to facilitate productive communications between the two of you.

Few successful people have worked for excellent bosses their entire career. In fact, the survey referenced in Chapter One found that only 14 percent of leaders are positive role models for their followers. Somewhere along the way, most are faced with dealing with bosses who do not share their values, who don't provide clear visions and who are incapable of positive relationships.

Jesus taught us how to deal with an arrogant boss in the parable of the persistent widow in Luke 18. In that parable, her "boss" neither feared God nor cared about the people. Jesus' direction was simple: *"Always pray and do not give up."*[13] Even when you choose to no longer work for someone, never give up your prayers for him.

Upward communication goes against organizational gravity and requires courage. *If you make communication a priority with your boss your relationship will improve, and you will achieve better results.*

A positive, productive working relationship with your leader is important for three reasons. One, your own job satisfaction. Two, your team depends upon you to support them and get results from your leader. And the final reason your relationship with your boss is important is because the better your understanding of your boss, the better you will be able to help them accomplish their goals.

The time you spend developing a positive relationship with your leader will yield improved performance and increased job satisfaction for you, your leader and those you lead.

COMMUNICATION WITH YOUR HEAVENLY FATHER

Your most important communication is with your Heavenly Father through continual prayer. When our communication with God breaks down, we are subjected to making decisions we do not want to make. *To be a follower of Jesus, prayer is essential to our happiness and success.*

The Bible provides explicit direction in our communication with our heavenly Father:

♦ Create dedicated time to pray, time when you can pray and listen to God's direction. Prayer is two-way communication between you and God. Take the time to listen to God's direction for you. *"Be still and know that I am God."*[14]

♦ Pray with an open Bible. Our direction from God comes from an intimate prayer life and our study of the Word. The Bible says, *"In quietness and trust is your strength."*[15]

♦ Pray whenever, wherever, and with whomever. The Bible says, *"Do not put out the Spirit's fire."*[16] The way to keep the fire burning is through an ongoing prayer life.

♦ Be specific in your prayers. When the blind beggar asked Jesus to have mercy on him, Jesus asked him, *"What do you want me to do for you?"* Jesus knew what the man wanted, but only after he specifically said, *"Lord, I want to see"*[17] did Jesus restore his sight.

Any day without spending time with the Father is a wasted day. If you are uncomfortable praying, pray more. There are no instant prayer warriors; you learn to pray by praying.

SUMMARY

Effective communication is critical to your success as a leader. Your ability to connect with people from different backgrounds and experiences is a talent to be nurtured in your daily leadership activities. Here are some suggestions:

♦ Be creative in your communication.

♦ Have a specific plan to communicate with your team and your leader.

♦ Focus on what you consider to be the main things that lead to success.

♦ Be in personal contact with your followers.

♦ Develop trust through your communication.

♦ Make communication with your heavenly Father your top priority.

Remember! The highest form of communication is your example. People hear what you say and how you say it, but people follow what they see you do. Be aware of the messages your actions are communicating!

It is up to you to decide how to speak to your people.
Make people who work for you feel important.
If you honor and serve them, they'll honor and serve you.
—Mary Kay Ash

CHAPTER SEVEN

OVERCOMING ADVERSITY

Consider it pure joy, my brothers, whenever you face trials of many kinds,
because you know that the testing of your faith develops perseverance.
— James 1:2-3

THE PRINCIPLE OF ADVERSITY

Leadership results improve to the extent
that the leader is able to overcome adversity.

A friend's mother has lost her short-term memory. One day over coffee, he was sharing an update on his mother's condition. "In a way," he said wryly, "my mother has reached an enviable point in her life."

My expression reflected my lack of understanding.

"Because," my friend continued, "every day she wakes up in a new world. Every problem has disappeared, every worry is left behind, every trouble is gone … because she can't remember."

Wouldn't it be great if every morning when we woke up, all the issues that existed the previous day were gone? Life would be a lot easier – there would be fewer headaches and a lot less of a drain on our leadership reservoir. Except for my friend's mother's condition, it rarely works that way.

Every person will face adversity – no one is immune. Adversity is a part of life ... and every person will be challenged with it at some point. Adversity is a test of our stability – our ability to endure, continue and survive. Solomon tells us in Proverbs 24:10, *"If you falter in times of trouble, how small is your strength."* There is nothing like adversity to reveal how strong we really are.

My greatest personal adversity challenge occurred several years ago. Within a span of six months, my wife Karen was diagnosed with a rare, aggressive cancer. My father passed away. And, I had open heart surgery. The pressure of facing those three major events almost simultaneously was nearly too much to bear. However, I learned firsthand that God's grace was sufficient and He was in control.

Karen is now an inspiration for many others battling cancer. My dad lived a full, wonderful life without suffering. And, I have learned to refocus my life on what is important!

When adversity invades our lives, we soon discover what we are made of – and what lies at the core of our character. Leaders must react to personal adversity as well as the adversity that their team encounters.

In a recent meeting of 20 highly successful people, the topic of adversity was discussed. They agreed that overcoming adversity was a critical turning point in their own personal success. But, not until everyone began sharing the adversity they had personally overcome did I realize how universal adversity is.

Within that group, people had faced cancer, suicide, divorce, loss of children, drug abuse, loss of spouse, significant health issues, bankruptcy and other areas of disappointments. Everyone there had faced a major crisis.

Is it surprising that Christian leaders – wonderful, God-fearing people – have problems just like everyone else?

Some of the adversities are beyond anyone's control, and some are self-inflicted. But, regardless of how or why the adversity occurred, every successful Christian leader has faced, attacked and conquered adversity somewhere along the way. Overcoming adversity is one area in which every leader's character is put to the test.

PEOPLE, ADVERSITY, GROWTH

Cyclist Lance Armstrong or the late Christopher Reeve would probably be mentioned often as examples of individuals who chose to avoid the muck of self-pity as they challenged adversity and went on with life, becoming a voice for many and examples for many more.

But, look around … and you probably don't have to look far to find examples of people who have chosen to attack and conquer adversity through their faith and perseverance. They may not get the national attention Armstrong or Reeve received, but their challenges were just as dramatic.

One of the most positive and enthusiastic people I know is a friend of mine named Melissa. When you meet Melissa, she appears to have it all – a terrific personality, good looks, smart, fun and successful.

What is not apparent is that Melissa is a winner when it comes to conquering adversity. Five years ago, Melissa was a homemaker, taking care of her three-year-old autistic child and a newborn – a challenging, full time job.

One day without warning, Melissa's life suddenly changed. Without any explanation, her husband announced he was leaving. He walked out the door and never turned back, leaving Melissa and the children with the house and the bills ... and he moved in with one of Melissa's good friends.

Losing her husband and her friend and being left to pick up the pieces without financial or emotional support was enough to handle. But, Melissa's adversity was even greater because she had left her career four years earlier to stay home and have a family – she did not even have any income.

Melissa's easiest and most logical choice would have been to become mired in self-pity, bitterness and hatred over the unfair situation and focus her anger toward her husband and friend – who would blame her?

Some say adversity grinds you down. Others say it polishes you up ... it depends on what you're made of and how you choose to respond to the adversity that comes your way.

Adversity polished Melissa. One at a time, she picked up the shattered pieces and continued to move forward with her life. Her trip has not been easy, but she would not allow adversity to destroy her, her children or their dreams.

Today, Melissa is a successful graphic designer (she designed this book) as well as a tremendous inspiration to me, and others, because she chose to do the best she could with an unfair situation.

Choice is power, and when confronted with adversity we can choose to see the positive alternatives and rise from the ashes to become even better than we were before – or we can choose to sit and savor our pitiful circumstances for the rest of our lives.

LEADING THROUGH ADVERSITY

Not all adversity is personal. Leaders face adversity within their workgroup as well. Excellent leaders stay in tune with team members and are seldom blind-sided by major problems. As the Bible says, *"A sensible man watches for problems ahead and prepares to meet them. The simpleton never looks, and suffers the consequences."*[1]

Adversity within workgroups can be devastating unless it is addressed quickly and fairly. The successful leader has the ability to immediately recognize adversity and is armed with the courage necessary to address a problem before it becomes a catastrophe.

The Bible provides explicit direction concerning adversity.

Moses was faced with a situation that most leaders face somewhere along the way. In Exodus 17:4 he cries to the Lord, *"What am I to do with these people? They are almost ready to stone me."*

Most of us can relate to that. Things might not be going as planned. Our people are unhappy and may be ready to revolt. The Lord directed Moses to stay ahead (focused), take some helpers (get the right team), and go (execute the plan). Just when the followers were at the point of revolting, God provided for Moses.

It is human nature to dislike adversity. Working through adversity is hard work. By definition, adversity means that something is not right, and unless the situation is personally affecting them, most people would rather do anything than attack adversity. But, if the problem is affecting them, they want it fixed immediately!

In Proverbs, we learn how to deal with adversity:

♦ First, get the facts: *"He who answers without listening, that is his folly and his shame."*

♦ Second, try new things: *"The heart of the discerning acquires knowledge, the ears of the wise seek it out."*

♦ Third, listen to both sides of the issue: *"The first to present his case seems right, till another comes forward and questions him."*[2]

Jesus taught that adversity could be a test of our faith. In the midst of a storm, when Jesus was asleep in the boat with his disciples, the disciples panicked saying, *"We are going to drown." They asked their leader, "Don't you care?"*[3] They imagined the worst and lost their faith in the power of the one with them. Jesus said, *"Why are you still afraid? Do you still have no faith?"* Even after all the miracles they had seen Jesus perform, when faced with adversity they still were not sure he could solve their problem.

Cain and Abel were the first examples of adversity within a family.[4] Cain made bad choices because his anger and emotions were out of control. Adversity will not be overcome while you are angry. With anger, you are guaranteed to make bad choices with permanent consequences, setting the stage for additional bad choices.

THE LEADER'S RESPONSIBILITY

People will always have conflicts, the team will always have problems and the leader will always be needed to help solve them.

Your first challenge, as a leader, is to look at the situation positively and to recognize that your value is in finding acceptable solutions –

which requires time, energy and focus. Norman Vincent Peale said, "Positive thinking is how you think about a problem. Enthusiasm is how you feel about a problem. The two together determine what you do about a problem."

VERTICAL OR LATERAL THINKER

Your role is to be positive and enthusiastic while searching to find workable solutions, but it is also important to know what kind of problem solver you are.

Oxford's Edward deBono suggests using "detours and reversals," anything that will give us a different angle on trying to solve problems. To illustrate, he tells this story:

A well-known company had relocated its headquarters to a new skyscraper and discovered the builder had not put in enough elevators. Employees were becoming increasingly more vocal about long waits for the elevators, especially at both ends of the working day.

Company leadership convened a wide cross-section of the staff and asked them to solve the problem. The group came up with the following four possible solutions:

1. Increase the speed of the elevators.

2. Stagger work hours to reduce elevator demand at both ends of the day.

3. Install mirrors around entrances to all elevators.

4. Add a new elevator.

Following much consideration, the company opted for the third solution – and it worked.

"People became so preoccupied with looking at themselves or at others, they no longer noticed the wait for the elevator," deBono explained. "The problem was not so much the lack of elevators as the impatience of the employees."

If you chose the first, second or fourth solutions, you are a "vertical" or traditional thinker. If you chose Solution #3, you are a "lateral thinker." The vertical thinker takes the narrow view; the lateral thinker has a broader view.

When problems arrive in your workgroup, think outside your normal view and look for alternative ways to arrive at a solution.

MOLEHILLS AND MOUNTAINS!

In organizations today, the majority of adversity inside organizations involves interpersonal conflicts within the workgroup. The Bible says, *"If a house is divided against itself that house cannot stand."*[5]

These conflicts cannot be neglected. Few work themselves out without third-party interventions, but the longer problems are allowed to continue, the more likely they are to spread through the workgroup and, ultimately, throughout the organization.

What happens if you ignore a problem?

Most mountain-size adversity began as a molehill. Ignoring a molehill does not make it go away – it just continues to get larger and larger. Ignore it long enough and, eventually, it becomes a mountain that will block the path to where you are going.

There is a conflict resolution concept called the 1-10-100 rule or the "molehills to mountains rule." Loosely translated, the longer a conflict exists without being identified or addressed, the more expensive and time consuming it is to fix.

You can apply the molehills-to-mountains rule in many situations –
an adversarial conflict between two team members, a billing
discrepancy with your customer, a quality slippage, or a simple lack
of communication.

Each of these issues has two things in common:

1) They negatively impact people and overall team performance.

2) Rather than fix themselves, they "snowball" over time.

For example, if a conflict is solved quickly and efficiently between
two people, it can be solved with the equivalent of one unit of
time, money or resources. That same problem – if it is not
addressed and allowed to spread into a workgroup – will require
the equivalent of 10 units of time, money or resources to solve
because more emotions and perceptions must now be addressed
since the problem has spread.

If the problem is allowed to work through the organization or into
the customer base, it will then require at least 100 units of
measurement to solve. That is 100 times what it would have cost to
solve the same problem in the beginning.

You have probably seen minor situations become major catastrophes
because the problem was not addressed. Solve problems before they
become a disaster!

An old proverb says you should "never leave a nail sticking up where
you find it." When you apply this old proverb to organizational
leadership, the translation is: Don't ignore problems. Address them
as soon as they come up, because problems will not go away on
their own.

GET THE FACTS

The key to conflict resolution is to understand what the problem really is. We have all seen two people in furious disagreement over what they think the other one is thinking.

The Bible says, *"Get the facts at any price, and hold on tightly to all the good sense you can get."*[6] Sometimes it requires all your energy just to hold on tightly to your good sense while you are getting the facts. This illustration is a story told by a college professor about a letter from his student to her parents:[7]

Dear Mother and Dad,

Since I left for college I have been remiss in writing to you. I am really sorry for my thoughtlessness in not writing before. I will bring you up to date now, but before you read on, please sit down. You are not to read any further unless you are sitting down. Okay?

Well, then, I am getting along pretty well now. The skull fracture I got when I jumped out of the window of my dormitory when it caught fire shortly after my arrival here is pretty well healed. I spent only two weeks in the hospital, and now I can see almost normally and get those sick headaches only once a day.

Fortunately, the fire in the dormitory (and my jump) was witnessed by an attendant at the gas station near the dorm, and he was the one who called the fire department and the ambulance. He also visited me in the hospital, and since I had nowhere to live because of the burnt-out dormitory, he was kind enough to invite me to share his apartment with him. It's really just a basement room, but it's kind of cute.

He is a fine boy, and we have fallen deeply in love and are planning to get married. We haven't set the exact date yet, but it will be before my pregnancy begins to show. Yes, Mother and Dad, I am pregnant. I know how much you are looking forward to being grandparents, and I know you will welcome the baby and give it the same love and devotion and tender care you gave me when I was a child.

The reason for the delay in our marriage is that my boyfriend has a minor infection, which prevents us from passing our premarital blood tests, and I carelessly caught it from him. But, I know that you will welcome him into our family with open arms. He is kind and, although not well educated, he is ambitious. I know your often-expressed tolerance will not permit you to be bothered by that.

Now that I have brought you up to date, I want to tell you that there was no dormitory fire. I did not have a skull fracture. I was not in the hospital. I am not pregnant. I am not engaged. I am not infected, and there is no boyfriend in my life. However, I am getting a D in History and an F in Biology, and I wanted you to see these grades in their proper perspectives.

Your loving daughter,

Susie

Remember: Hold on tightly to all good sense while you are getting the facts! Many interpersonal problems in organizations develop because the leader has failed to grasp the facts contributing to the problem and is focused on solving the wrong problem.

PERSONAL CONFLICTS WITH YOUR TEAM

There is one exception to the "solve the problem now" or molehills to mountains rule, and that exception is when you are personally involved in a conflict. Then, it is best to put time between the situation and your response instead of trying to solve the problem immediately.

Every leader, regardless of tenure or success, will be faced with responding to adversity between himself and someone on his team. No one is immune to this uncomfortable position. However, few will be faced with a situation as challenging as this one:

While David and his warriors were away to fight a battle, the enemy attacked and burned their village. The enemy also took captive the soldiers' wives, sons, and daughters. Imagine a scene so horrible that these strong warriors *"wept aloud until they had no strength left to weep."*

The men blamed their leader, David, for their tragic loss and talked of stoning him. You can almost feel David's pain, because his own family had also been captured and now his own soldiers had turned on him.

Yet, even in this tragic situation, David kept his cool and put some time and space between the conflict and his response. He left to seek a quiet place to sort through the issues, and he *"found strength in the Lord his God."* During his time of prayer and solitude, he was able to find a course of action that led to a solution.[8]

There is much wisdom to the practice of "sleeping on a problem" when you are personally involved in the situation. Follow David's example the next time you are faced with a personal conflict with a follower. Keep your cool, don't panic, go to a quiet place and seek God's direction for solutions to your problem. Then follow the Bible's guidance: *"Everyone should be quick to listen, slow to speak and slow to become angry. For man's anger does not bring about the righteous life that God desires."*[9] Keep your cool!

HOW TO CONQUER PERSONAL ADVERSITY

Chris Novak, my friend and author of *Conquering Adversity*[10] (a book I think every person walking this earth needs to read), is a great example of making the choice to move forward and keep your faith, even after an unimaginable tragedy.

Chris, a happily married family man with one child and another on the way, received a phone call in the middle of just another day at the office informing him that his wife and unborn son had been killed in an automobile accident.

That call would change his life forever. No one would have blamed him for being bitter and consumed with the unfairness of life.

Yet, after grieving this tragic loss, Novak chose to take the lessons of catastrophe and create opportunities from the alternatives his life now offered.

In *Conquering Adversity*, he shares how he was able to move forward, saying, "Life is not fair, so don't expect it to be. Regardless of how bleak the situation appears there are alternatives that will help you move forward ... if you choose to see them."

He suggests that you attack adversity by doing the following:

1. **Affirmation** – Acknowledge what is and what is not lost. It is natural in times of extreme duress to believe that everything is lost. We have to acknowledge that, even in the greatest of tragedies, we do not lose everything. The fear of moving forward is the power that adversity has over us. Ultimately, we have to make the decision to move ahead. (*"Come to me, all you who are weary and burdened, and I will give you rest. Take my yoke upon you and learn from me, for I am gentle and humble in heart, and you will find rest for your souls. For my yoke is easy and my burden is light."*)[11]

2. **Expectation** – Adversity attacks our vision, limits our sights and blinds us with the challenges of the moment. After adversity attacks us, we have to make the choice to pull ourselves up, avoid the "why" trap and move forward with positive expectations. (*"No eye has seen, no ear has heard, no mind has conceived what God has prepared for those who love him."*)[12]

3. **Communication** – To conquer adversity, we have to allow God to help through others. Many times we struggle by ourselves; dealing with adversity when a prayer or someone just a phone call away would provide the answer that would have moved us forward. People want to help, but most of the time they have to be invited. (*"For everyone who asks receives; he who seeks finds; and to him who knocks, the door will be open."*)[13]

4. **Locomotion** – One of the greatest dangers in facing adversity is that we panic, freeze and stop, because we perceive the roadblocks, barriers or mountains in our lives as insurmountable. People respond better to crisis when they maximize their forward motion. We have to keep moving forward. (*"Let us not become weary in doing good, for at the proper time we will reap a harvest if we do not give up."*)[14]

5. **Collaboration** – Most challenges we face cannot be overcome alone. We should not attempt to meet adversity with no one to support us. Collaboration is about the people we take with us on our journey forward. (*"Blessed are those who mourn, for they will be comforted."*)[15]

6. **Celebration** – Celebration feeds our positive energy and our sense of hope. It nourishes our spirits, refreshes our attitudes and gives us strength to fight off the inevitable attacks of

negativism and fear that accompany severe adversity. (*"For I am convinced that neither death nor life, neither angels nor demons, neither the present nor the future, not any powers, neither height nor depth, nor anything else in all creation, will be able to separate us from the love of God that is in Christ Jesus our Lord."*)[16]

Chris Novak's metamorphosis serves as an exquisite model for all of us about how to use catastrophe as a catalyst in our lives. He provides evidence that there are alternatives even in life's most painful shadows; but Novak is the first to admit that the options for his life became suddenly more plentiful as he began to know himself — for the first time — within the context of his devastating loss.

SUMMARY

It is the leader's role to clear a path to success by overcoming adversity. Whatever adversity you are facing personally or professionally, you are not the first person to face your problem. Other people have overcome the challenge that is consuming your thoughts, energy and hopes. Remember, from the moment you embark on your journey to overcome adversity that God will guide you and provide you the strength to win if you seek His help. He will be with you through the deep valleys, the raging waters and the consuming fires … He will never, ever leave you or forsake you.

Adversity causes some men to break, others to break records.
—William Arthur Ward

CHAPTER EIGHT

OPTIMISM

Whatever things are true, whatsoever things are honest, whatsoever things are just, whatsoever things are pure, whatsoever things are lovely, whatsoever things are of good report, if there be any virtue, and if there be any praise, think on these things.
— Philippians 4:8 (KJV)

THE PRINCIPLE OF OPTIMISM

Leadership results improve in direct proportion to the self-concept and optimism of the leader.

Optimism is a courageous state of mind, one that comes from a person's desire, effort and choice to accept, and make the best of, difficult situations. Certainly, the road of optimism is not without potholes ... and, that is especially true for those in leadership positions.

If you lead long enough, you'll undoubtedly face setbacks and unexpected events that have the potential to be devastating. The optimistic leader is a leader with faith who recognizes that defeat is a temporary setback — isolated to a given situation.

"An optimist sees an opportunity in every calamity; a pessimist sees a calamity in every opportunity." That was Winston Churchill's view – and the following story illustrates his point, depicting how optimistic people potential that others fail to realize:

Two researchers were independently dispatched to one of the world's least developed countries by a large shoe manufacturer. Their task was to assess the business possibilities within that country.

When the first report came back to the manufacturer's headquarters, the message read: "No market here. Nobody wears shoes!" A few days later, the second report came back from the other researcher. It read: "Great market here. Nobody wears shoes!"

Optimism is the result of a person's desire and effort to accept a difficult situation and make that situation the best possible – no matter what. All leaders are faced with setbacks and unexplainable events that are unexpected and sometimes destructive.

Because of today's pace of life, things happen that shove us onto unfamiliar paths that test our faith. It is easy to be optimistic when things are going well, but the effective leader remains optimistic and searches for the best, even in times of stress and uncertainty. No one enjoys the unknown, but regardless of the struggles confronting the team, the optimistic leader expects the best possible outcome. It is a fact that what you expect influences what happens down the road.

Paul reflected in 2 Corinthians 7:4, *"I have great confidence in you. I take great pride in you. I am greatly encouraged; in all our troubles my joy knows no bounds."*

Optimistic leaders refuse to waste their energy worrying about situations over which they have no control. Author Charles Dickens advised, "Reflect upon your present blessings, of which every man has many – not on your past misfortunes, of which all men have some."

COMBAT THE ENEMIES

Great leaders approach every difficulty with optimism and determination.

Two of optimism's greatest enemies are worry and the negative emotions that often accompany anxiety. Worry creates fear, drains your energy, prevents you from achieving your potential and obstructs your team from obtaining their goals. Not much happens – good or otherwise – when you are paralyzed with worry.

Most of what we worry about is beyond our control to change. What we do control is our action to keep the worry from happening. *The antidote to worry is to make the decision to take action to prevent the worry from happening.*

Jesus was explicit in his teachings about worry. In the Sermon on the Mount[1] He asked, *"Who of you by worrying can add a single hour to his life?"* Later He said, *"I tell you, do not worry about your life."* Jesus knew the negative effects of worry. It damages your health, consumes your thoughts, and it paralyzes your decision-making process.

In our society today, the average person worries about:

♦ Things that will never happen – 40% of the time

♦ Things about the past that can't be changed – 30% of the time

♦ Things about criticism by others, mostly untrue – 12% of the time

♦ Health, which gets worse with stress – 10% of the time

♦ Real problems that will be faced – 8% of the time

A leader consumed by worry cannot effectively lead at home, church or the office. Paul taught us not to worry about anything, but to pray about everything: *"Do not be anxious about anything, but in everything, by prayer and petition, with thanksgiving, present your request to God."*[2] To worry less, you need to pray more.

In the parable of the four soils, Jesus taught about those that hear the word of God but *"as they go their way become choked by life's worries, riches, and pleasures and they do not mature."*[3] Worry indicates a lack of faith and consumes the energy and optimism that are ours through God.

Avoiding worry isn't easy, but it can be done.

Leading people is not always easy, either. In some instances, it is a real struggle! All followers have different personalities and are motivated differently. They have personal problems, financial issues, concerns about children, and plenty of other distractions. And, while you are leading others, you still have your own personal problems!

Jesus acknowledged that we do struggle with our responsibilities, and He provided for our relief. *"Come to me, all you who are weary and burdened, and I will give you rest. Take my yoke upon you and learn from me, for I am gentle and humble in heart, and you will find rest for your souls. For my yoke is easy and my burden is light."*[4] Notice that He did not promise us a life without burdens, but He did provide a way to handle the burdens we carry.

To combat worry, follow these steps:

♦ **Get the facts** – Most worry is based on false assumptions. Things that we fear will happen, as opposed to what is actually happening. Get the real facts, and try not to worry about the fears that drain your energy.

♦ **Consider the worst possible outcome** – If your worry is among the small percent over which you have control, what will be the effect if it does come to pass? Once you discover the worst possible outcome, you will often find that it is not as bad as you thought. You can probably live with it even though you may have to make some changes. Your stress comes from not understanding the worst possible outcome and allowing you to deal with it.

♦ **Begin to improve on the worst possible outcome** – Create a plan that will begin purposeful action to ensure that the worst does not happen. It is difficult to worry about things you are working diligently to improve. Again, the antidote to worry is taking action to prevent something from happening.

♦ **Pray about it and let it go** – A Barnam study revealed that only 31 percent of Americans pray daily. That means that a lot of people are trying to carry their burdens alone. As Paul said, don't worry about anything, pray about everything. If you have done everything you can to prevent the worry from happening, and you have asked for God's help, let it go. Your worrying is not helping anyone or anything. In fact, it is probably making you and those around you miserable.

WHAT ABOUT THOSE NEGATIVE EMOTIONS?

The second enemy of optimism is negative emotions. Everyone has negative emotions and must create a way to minimize the damage they can cause. Negative emotions – such as hate, fear, doubt, jealousy, self-pity, anger, and resentment – will never add to your leadership success.

To combat negative emotions, try these six steps:

♦ **Face the reality of the negative emotion** – What you are experiencing is real. You are feeling its effects, and it is having a negative impact on your leadership. Don't deny it; do something about it.

♦ **Do not criticize yourself** – you are human. Beating yourself up for expressing human emotions creates more negativity and does nothing to solve the problem or make you a more effective leader.

♦ **Do not blame anyone** – Placing the blame will not solve the problem or cause the negative emotion to disappear. Avoid blaming anyone for anything. Blame always focuses on the past and does not do anything to solve your current problem.

♦ **Accept responsibility** – The faster you can learn to say, "I am responsible for my negative emotion of _____," the more quickly you can be productive again. Responsibility focuses on the future and is the beginning of turning the negative emotion into a positive action.

♦ **Ask for forgiveness** – If you have any unfinished business contributing to the negative feelings, go to the person and ask him/her to forgive you. This action will release the guilt, anger, jealousy, etc., from you and allow you to go forward.

♦ **Pray about it** – Ask for God's forgiveness, accept His forgiveness, and be the positive, optimistic leader He wants you to be.

REMEMBER WHO IS IN CONTROL

In times when you and your people are struggling, and worry and negative emotions are consuming you, the way for the Christian leader to be optimistic is to *accept that God is in control*. I know! When my business was struggling to get off the ground and it seemed hopeless, I came home to my wife and threw myself a real pity party. Karen called that party off, saying it was obvious that God had provided in the past, and she knew that He would continue to provide. She said that I could not quit even if I wanted to. "You can only quit what you control, and God has control of our business."

She was right. Nothing in God's control is out of control. It was my job to use the talents I had been given to follow God's direction. I discovered that *it is difficult to worry while you are energetically working toward a plan!* That realization became a turning point. I changed my worry to optimism and began accepting whatever the Lord provides.

YOUR ATTITUDE MAKES A DIFFERENCE

A major difference between successful leaders and others is that successful leaders insist on reliving and recreating past success. They find ways to duplicate their success, even though the situation has changed. The unsuccessful insist on reliving their past failures and wind up duplicating those failures. Don't let your past eat your future.

A salesman moved into a new town and met an old-timer as he was leaving the bank. "I'm new to your town. What are the people like here?" the salesman asked.

"What were the people like in the town you came from?" the old-timer responded.

"Well, they were glum and negative and always complaining, and their glasses were always half-empty," the salesman replied.

"Hmmm," said the old-timer. "Sounds about like the people who live here."

A few weeks later, another person moved to the same town and met the same old-timer as he was leaving the same bank. "I'm new to your town. What are the people like here?" the newcomer asked.

"What were the people like in the town you came from?" the old-timer responded.

"Well, they were wonderful. They worked together in the neighborhood, helped each other out, and were always there to support us during tough times. We're going to miss them," the newcomer replied.

"Hmmm," said the old-timer. "I think you will like it here. That sounds about like the people who live here."

The old-timer's message? If you want to be around people who are positive and enthusiastic and eager to live life, your attitude has to be the same. If you think the people around you are glum and negative then you probably ought to check your own attitude, because it is probably glum and negative, too.

LOOK FOR YOUR BEST

Maintaining an optimistic outlook requires you to always *look for the best in yourself and others*. Many times, being positive about ourselves goes against our human nature. We are the most critical of ourselves. People are far more careful of what they say to others than what they say to themselves.

Typically, a large percent of our self-talk is negative – "I can't, I won't, we don't, no one," etc. Should we feel that way about ourselves? Certainly not – you are one of God's children. You are not inferior ... you're okay. The faster you accept that fact, the sooner you will be able to enjoy your leadership role.

Even when you are stressed to the max, maintain a positive attitude by being a champion at positive self-talk. Replace "I can't" with "I can"; "I won't" with "I will"; "we don't" with "we do"; and "no one" with "we are the ones." It will make a difference in how you feel about yourself and in your ability to be an effective leader.

SUMMARY

A pessimistic leader will eventually lead to disaster. Consistent, positive results are achieved only through consistent, positive leadership.

Here is Paul's advice on how to be an optimistic leader:

1. Don't dwell on your mistakes.
   "Forgetting what is behind and straining toward what is ahead, I press heavenward in Christ Jesus." Philippians 3:13-14

2. Think positive.
   "I can do everything through Him that gives me strength." Philippians 4:13

3. Throw away fear. Trust your instincts.
   "For God does not give us a spirit of timidity, but a spirit of power, of love, and of self discipline." 2 Timothy 1:7

4. Keep the dream alive. Don't abandon your aspirations.
   "I want to know Christ, and the power of his resurrection and the fellowship of sharing in his sufferings, becoming like him in his death." Philippians 3:10

Our happiness and ability to remain optimistic will never be achieved by obtaining what we perceive others to have. We control our outlook based on our ability to be thankful for our own situation ... whatever it might be.

If you are a Christian, your eternal worries are over! You are one of the few people on earth who know, without a doubt, that their future is secure. Ecclesiastes 3:11-12 says, *"He has made everything beautiful in its time. He has also set eternity in the hearts of men; yet they cannot fathom what God has done from beginning to end. I know that there is nothing better from men than to be happy and do good while they live."*

Enjoy the challenges of life and depend on God to meet your needs – that is how to remain optimistic regardless of what is going on around you!

Things turn out best for the people who
make the best of the way things turn out.
– John Wooden

CHAPTER NINE

POSITIVE CHANGE

So they shook their feet in protest against them and went to Iconium.
And the disciples were filled with joy and with the Holy Spirit.
— Acts 13:51-52

THE PRINCIPLE OF POSITIVE CHANGE

**Leadership results improve to the extent that the leader is
able to embrace change and accept responsibility for change.**

When Heraclitus uttered the words, "The only constant
is change" in 500 B.C., do you suppose he was
envisioning the warp-speed changes we face today?

Probably not! Nevertheless, leading people through change almost
2000 years ago, undoubtedly, came with its own unique set of
challenges and difficulties.

Humans inherently resist change in varying degrees ... and clearly,
the message of that ancient historical figure is: Get beyond the ways

of the past and present and start looking toward improvement in the future. Can we improve without changing something? Does improvement come from just wanting improvement?

Obviously, not. Author Max Dupree might have said it best: "In the end, it is important to remember that we cannot become what we need to be by remaining what we are."[1] Change is as natural as breathing, yet many seem to prefer to take their last breath rather than embrace change that can allow things to improve.

Change involves leaving your comfort zone to try something different – creating an opportunity to improve. Without change, we all get in a rut of doing the same things the same way. Why are we surprised when we achieve the same result by doing things the same way? That rut can eventually become a grave because the only difference between a rut and a grave is the depth.

The Bible helps us understand the process of changing. Many of the great heroes of the Bible went through major changes in their lives. The key to their successful change was that they were following God's will. If we are in God's will, change can lead to greater results than every imagined.

We have already discussed the change that took place in the life of Moses. He resisted and made excuses yet, because the change was God-directed, he became the leader of God's people.[2]

God told Abram, at the age of 75, to take a new direction. Following God's will, Abram left the security of his comfort zone and made a major change – even at age 75. He followed God and became the father of the Jewish people.[3]

Jesus changed people *who were willing to be changed.* Through their faith in Jesus, people who were considered unchangeable were changed – lepers, the demon-possessed and the diseased.

In more recent times, people have created positive change when something happened to redirect them. Levi Strauss was intent on panning for gold when he invented jeans to help the gold diggers whose flimsy clothing was shredded to rags after only a few days of work. Although he never made it to the gold, Strauss became wealthy during the California gold rush not by panning for gold but by responding to a need, accepting an unexpected opportunity and creating something positive.

John Pemberton was a pharmacist who experimented with various remedies to heal sore throats. He stumbled onto a syrup recipe that tasted good and was enjoyed by people, even though they were not ailing. That's how Coca-Cola began. John Pemberton took a completely different direction from the one he had planned.

LEARNING FROM THE MOUSE

Several years ago there was an experiment evaluating reaction to change. Four tubes were laid side by side on the floor. A cube of cheese was placed in the second tube. A mouse was then released and it immediately went to the first tube. Finding the tube empty, the mouse proceeded to the second tube. There he discovered and ate the cheese, which met his basic need for survival. The mouse then returned to his point of release.

The next day, the mouse followed the same routine by going to the empty first tube, eating cheese from the second tube and returning to his point of release. He repeated the same routine for several days.

Finally, realizing that he was wasting time by going to the first tube, the mouse began going directly to the second tube. He ate the cheese, met his need for survival and went back. This routine also continued for several days.

The next day, the people conducting the experiment moved the cheese to the third tube. The mouse went directly to the second tube where his needs had always been met, and there was no cheese. What do you think the mouse's response was? Did he go back to the first tube looking for the cheese? No. Did he go back to where he started? No. Did he go to the third tube searching for the cheese? No. He chose to stay in the second tube, where his need of survival had always been met, and wait for the cheese to come back to him.

If allowed, the mouse would have starved in the tube, waiting for the cheese instead of reacting to the change. Doesn't this sound like the reaction of some people we know? "Let's wait," they say. "We have always done it this way, and it has always worked in the past!"

Two points can be learned from this story:

First, if the situation changes – even if your needs have always been met and you are comfortable with the old way – react to the change. The second lesson from the mouse is that while your needs are being met, keep looking for ways to improve.

If you've lived more than two decades, you are well aware that things do change and things do improve. The telegraph will never return. VHS videotapes are almost a thing of the past. Black-and-white televisions will never come back. Manual typewriters are gone forever.

Change is not unique to technology. Look around. Look at the workplace ... or your family and friends. For me, traditions are important – especially our family traditions. But as my family has grown, we have had to make adjustments to our traditions. I can't worry about the changes, I have to adapt to changes.

If you are waiting for things to be like they used to be, you could wind up starving like the mouse or you may be just plain miserable. When situations change, don't sit and wait – always look for your cheese.

The second lesson to be learned from the mouse is that while your needs are being met, keep looking for ways to improve. A whole block of cheese could have been in the fourth tube, and the mouse would not have known because he was content having his basic needs met. The time to make improvement is while things are going well, and you are successful. Bottom line, when things are going well, keep looking for more cheese.

There's one absolute: Change is not going away. In fact, there will probably be more changes in technology, thoughts, people and the economy in the next 10 years than there have been in the last hundred years.

Be prepared. Your reaction to change and your leadership through change will have a major impact on your success and the success of your team.

WHY CHANGE IS RESISTED

Ever wonder why change is so difficult for people to embrace? Why can't people just accept that change will happen and that it can be good? The answer to both questions is the same: It is natural to resist change. Even the smallest of changes – like sitting at a different place at the dinner table – is resisted.

Most people enjoy stability and comfort. Change typically represents the opposite – discomfort and instability – and few people enjoy traveling into those regions. Just ask anyone trying to lose weight or give up smoking.

Regardless of how anyone feels about it, change is necessary for improvement. Someone once said: "Insanity is doing the same thing the same way you have always done it and expecting different results." Believe it! We have all experienced this kind of insanity at one time or another.

It is important to understand that people will resist change, primarily for five reasons:

1. *The change is out of their control – it represents the unknown.* They did not create or ask for the change. When people feel they are not in control, they become stressed and begin to resist.

   To eliminate the stress, *the leader must earn the team's trust long before the change occurs.* Your responsibility is to develop trust from Day One and prepare for the time when you ask your team to leave their comfort zone. Leading with integrity, communicating consistent messages, listening to employee concerns, and treating them with dignity and respect all add to your trust account.

2. *People do not understand why they are changing.* Without understanding why a change is being made, emotions tied to the old way of doing things are difficult to loosen. People have to understand why change is necessary before they can

be willing to let go of the past. Even if they do not agree, they will accept change more rapidly if they know why the change is occurring.

Your chances for successful change improve significantly when you *involve your team in the change process*. Inform them of the options and provide them the opportunity to be involved in analyzing the alternatives and creating the new plan. The more people you involve, the more ownership of the change your people will have.

If the change must happen and you control only the delivery of the message, *get support from your informal group leaders* before announcing the change. Ask for their involvement as you deliver the message. Their vocal support can make the difference in the acceptance of the change. Seeking their help builds their confidence and trust in you when the change is announced.

3. ***They succeeded the old way.*** In every organization, there is always a group of people who have excelled under the old conditions. Therefore, they don't feel the need to change even though it may eventually make them more efficient – and make their work easier. Rarely is there a strong group of defenders of new ways to counter those in opposition, so you can wind up with a group of strong resisters and a group of lukewarm (at best) supporters – both of whom you must lead and influence. Not an easy job.

  Talk with these folks and acknowledge their past successes. Let them know how important they are to you and the team. Tell them you need their help ... you need them to assume leadership roles in making the change happen.

4. ***They feel incapable of change.*** Changes in technology create fear for two reasons: because people are not confident they

can learn the new technology and because they are threatened by the change. The leader's role is to create confidence in his people and their ability to adjust to the change.

You create confidence by leading your people through the change. Your total commitment and your actions will be what they remember the most. Delivering inconsistent messages will rapidly destroy the trust you have built, and the change will be resisted.

5. **People think the price they have to pay outweighs the reward.** Be aware. They may think the change is not worth the discomfort. Then, if they do not understand the result or like what they see, they will do anything to make the change fail.

You can help determine your team's enthusiasm for the change by focusing on the result while you are working through the current trials.

Did you ever walk into a movie, only to see the last ten minutes of the show as the hero and heroine head to their life of happiness? All you see is the outcome. But if you watch the movie from the beginning, your perception is completely different because you know what happens in the end. Your stress level is down, you can relax and you can enjoy the trials along the way knowing that everything will be okay.

As you lead your people through changes, keep focused on the result. Talk about the rewards and see change as a leadership challenge. You do not necessarily have to like the change, but you have to respect it.

Let go of the past and move forward.

CHANGE LEADS TO IMPROVEMENT

Remember your first computer? I remember mine. It was given to me while I worked at FedEx. At the time, I could not understand why I needed a computer … I had a secretary and received all the information I needed. I was convinced computers were for nerds!

Not long after that, I remember seeing a woman talking on a cell phone in the grocery store. Why would anyone need a telephone in the grocery store? That question has not crossed my mind since.

Well, I am not the only person who couldn't see the significance of change. Think of what our lives would be like without the changes resulting after these predictions:

Everything that can be invented has been invented.
Charles Duell, Commissioner of Patents, 1899

Television won't be able to hold on to any market it captures after the first six months. People will soon get tired of staring at a plywood box every night.
Darrell Zanuck, Twentieth Century Fox, 1946

I think there is a world market for about five computers.
Thomas J. Watson, IBM, 1943

With over fifteen types of foreign cars already on sale here, the Japanese auto industry isn't likely to carve out a big share of the market for itself.
Business Week, 1968

There is no reason for any individual to have a computer in his home.
Kenneth Olson, founder, Digital Equipment, 1977

Think of all of the fabulous technological advancements that have taken place since these predictions. Those changes involved leaders who were able to share their vision with others to create an exciting end result.

The changes we lead our people through today might not have a dramatic effect on the history of mankind, but they can have a positive impact on the lives of the people involved in the change.

SUMMARY

Leading people through change is taxing. It is stressful. It often causes us to reach deeper within ourselves to achieve the results we know can be achieved.

We may meet resistance at every point in the process but as a leader, our job is to stay at least one step ahead of the resisters.

When leading through change, keep this Scripture in mind: *"Let us not become weary of doing good, for at the proper time we will reap a harvest if we do not give up."*[4]

Change is here to stay. Embrace change because when you stop changing, you stop improving.

"One of the great discoveries a man makes, one of his great surprises, is to find he can do what he was afraid he couldn't do."
–Henry Ford

PART THREE

THE INVESTMENT PRINCIPLES

EMPOWERMENT ♦ COURAGE
EXAMPLE ♦ PREPARATION

*The moment you make self-development and people development a priority
is the moment your results will begin to improve dramatically.*

CHAPTER TEN

EMPOWERMENT

Give and it shall be given to you; good measure, pressed down, and shaken together, and running over, shall men give into your bosom.
– Luke 6:38 (KJV)

THE PRINCIPLE OF EMPOWERMENT

Leadership results improve when you provide your team with the opportunity to accept total ownership of their work.

In *Flight of the Buffalo*,[1] authors James Belasco and Ralph Stayer write of the day they discovered the power of empowering their people:

"Then one day I got it. What I really wanted in the organization was a group of responsible, interdependent workers similar to a flock of geese. I could see the geese flying in their 'V' formation, the leader changing frequently, with different geese taking the lead. I saw every goose being responsible for getting itself to wherever the gaggle was going, changing roles whenever necessary, alternating as a leader, a follower or a scout. And when the task changed, the geese would be responsible for changing the structure of the group to accommodate, similar to the geese that fly in a 'V' but land in waves. I could see each goose being a leader.

"Then I saw clearly that the biggest obstacle to success was my picture of a loyal herd of buffalo waiting for me, the leader, to tell them what to do. I knew I had to change the pictures to become a different kind of leader, so everyone could become a leader."

RELEASING CONTROL

The definition of "empowerment" is to give somebody power or authority and to inspire someone with a sense of confidence or self-esteem. While everyone might say they would want the result of empowerment as defined, most of the time it is not as simple as giving power and inspiring someone's self esteem.

When today's enlistees join the military, they go through basic training. Anyone who has been through it can tell you – it's hard.

If they go on to join a special operations unit, the training is even harder. It lasts many months and includes extreme challenges – like Hell Week.

Hell Week typically lasts five days or more. You get a total of four hours of sleep a day, run long distances, endure bad weather or cold water for long periods, stay afloat with hands and feet bound and crawl through muddy courses with explosions all around you.

When you fall into your bunk with every joint screaming and your head spinning, someone wakes you, and it starts all over again. Only the most determined try to join these elite units and of those who dare, four in five drop out before training ends.

Those who make it through are among the most determined and dangerous people in the world. As they've pushed beyond the limits of their endurance, they find they can do things they once thought impossible. They learn they can keep going even when they're hungry, hurting and exhausted. They learn to say "no" to their own bodies and to keep going no matter what. They gain confidence that, even under the worst conditions against the deadliest enemies, they can still accomplish their mission. They are empowered.

Much like Special Forces personnel, leaders use empowerment to force their teams out of their comfort zones, place trust in others, and relinquish control. **No one will achieve long-term excellence by working on his own personal island.** Long-term success requires you, the leader, to draw upon a wide range of experiences from yourself and your people.

Along with empowering the people to do the job is the leader's need to understand and accept that people must have freedom to learn from their failures, as well as their successes.

JETHRO'S LESSONS

Moses discovered that he could not do everything himself. Out of desperation, he went to his father-in-law, Jethro, for advice. Jethro could see Moses was trying to do everything for his people – a mistake almost all leaders make in their careers. Maybe Moses was afraid to let go of his control or just didn't know what to do, but things were not working for him.

Written approximately 3,500 years ago, Exodus 18:17-27 teaches us the concept of improved results through empowerment, and

LEADERSHIP ... *Biblically Speaking*

Jethro's advice is just as applicable today as it was when he gave advice to Moses:

♦ *"What you are doing is not good—you will wear yourself out. The work is too heavy for you. You can't do everything by yourself."* Every successful leader learns that asking others to share the leadership role is best for everybody. The long-term results won't be as good as they could be if you try to do everything yourself.

♦ *"Listen to me."* Jethro wanted to help. I get the feeling he had been waiting for the right opportunity to contribute. Most men of wisdom and experience want to share that wisdom but will share only when asked. Successful leaders seek out mentors and learn from the people who have worked their way through the challenges they are facing.

♦ *"Be an example to them. Teach them and show them the way to live."* Jethro advised Moses to provide his people the tools to be successful, to lead them by example, to teach them what he knew and allow them to do things their way – not by doing everything for them.

♦ *"Select capable men to anoint as officials. Men who fear God are trustworthy and honest."* Jethro told Moses to find people he could trust and people who shared the same values. The ability of the men Moses appointed was important, but more important was choosing men of integrity to help lead the people.

♦ *"Select capable men from all the people."* Jethro was telling Moses to have diversity in his appointed leaders. The more diversity you have, the more effectively the team will function. Combining the experiences of people with different backgrounds will provide you with better information to make decisions.

♦ *"Let them bring the difficult cases to you and let them solve the simple cases. This will lighten your load because you share it with your people."* Jethro was directing Moses to spend his time doing what he did best and to allow his people to do the rest.

Jethro predicted that, *"Moses would be able to stand the strain and all your people would go home satisfied."*[2] His advice is sound: Recognize that you need your followers' help, teach them how to help and surround yourself with God-loving, trustworthy and honest people. Then empower them to solve their own problems, and intervene only when problems dictate your involvement. This will lighten your load and provide others a chance to grow.

JESUS' EXAMPLE

Jesus knew he, alone, could not do all that needed to be done so he chose his disciples and empowered them to do what needed to be done. He gave them power and authority, instructing them to *"drive out demons, cure diseases, and preach the kingdom of God."*[3] Jesus told his disciples what they were to do, what to take with them and how to handle the tough times. They were prepared to do what needed to be done.

Jesus had the power to do whatever he desired. He could have taught through power, but He chose to teach through love. Jesus had power over nature, over spirits, over disease and death,[4] yet He chose to use power only when that power brought about good for others. *His example was to lead others through love, not power.*

AREAS OF EXCELLENCE

We all have different gifts, and the Bible says, *"Each one should use whatever gift he has received to serve others, faithfully administering God's grace in its various forms."*[5] Whatever talents we have been given, we are to use them at home, school and work to glorify God.

In your area of excellence, things come easy to you. You enjoy the tasks and you have a talent with which few people are blessed. To be effective, you should be spending the majority of your time working where you are the most productive.

Your leadership effectiveness is measured by the results your followers accomplish. If Jesus chose not to do it all by himself, why should we think we can do it all by ourselves?

The Bible illustrates the effective use of teamwork in Romans 12:4: *"Just as each of us has one body with many members, and these members do not all have the same function, so in Christ we who are many form one body, and each member belongs to all the others. We have different gifts, according to the grace given us. If a man's gift is prophesying, let him use it in proportion to his faith. If it is serving, let him serve; if it is teaching, let him teach; if it is encouraging, let him encourage; if it is contributing to the needs of others, let him give generously; if it is leadership, let him govern diligently; if it is to show mercy, let him do it cheerfully."*

The best employees are normally those who are working on tasks they have selected in a field they really enjoy. Hire people who sincerely want the freedom to succeed. Empower your trusted associates to do the job by providing them with predetermined guidelines, and hold them accountable for the results.

WHEN NOT TO EMPOWER

Used correctly, empowerment will improve productivity and morale. However, you are flirting with disaster if you try to empower every decision or every team member.

Why? Because many situations are not empowerable. In fact, there are at least four areas you should never delegate:

1. Hiring your staff

2. Planning the strategy

3. Evaluating direct reports

4. Recognizing/rewarding performance

Before you automatically empower people, evaluate the situation and your people to avoid empowering their failure. Empowerment is effective only when your people are adequately prepared to handle the situation!

THE LEADER'S CHALLENGE

One of the greatest challenges for most leaders is to learn how to release control. Your challenge is to trust the people you have hired to get the results, even when their methods are different from yours. If you have hired and trained the right people for the job, and if they have the desire to do the job right, let go and give them the control. They will probably achieve results doing it in a way even better than the way you would have done it.

Empowerment is never successful without accountability.

Jesus made his disciples accountable after they were empowered: *"When they returned they reported to Jesus what they had done."*[6]

When you empower your people, follow Jesus' example! Train them, give specific instructions, let them know how to react to tough times, give them the freedom to be successful their way and hold them accountable for their results.

"Leadership: The art of getting someone else to do something you want done because he wants to do it."
— Dwight Eisenhower

Jethro's Eight Steps of Empowering Leadership
(*Exodus 18:17-27*)

1. Recognize that doing everything yourself is not good.

2. Understand your role as leader.

3. Listen to mentors with experience and wisdom.

4. Train your followers to become leaders.

5. Be an example to your people.

6. Select leaders who share your values and are capable of influencing others.

7. Select leaders with different backgrounds and experiences.

8. Intervene only when needed and hold your leaders accountable.

Chapter Eleven

COURAGE

And be not conformed to this world; but be ye transformed by the renewing of your mind, that ye may prove what is that good, and acceptable, and perfect will of God.
– Romans 12:2 (KJV)

THE PRINCIPLE OF COURAGE

Leadership results improve in proportion to the leader's courage to address issues affecting his team.

What is courage?

The dictionary tells us the word "courage" comes from the French "coeur," which means heart. Courage is "the attitude of facing and dealing with anything recognized as dangerous, difficult, or painful instead of withdrawing from it." The second definition is "the quality of being fearless or brave."

The relationship between courage and fear is interesting. For some, courage means not feeling fear at all. Some have suggested that men, in particular, interpret it this way. We raise our boys to think they shouldn't feel fear at all — that there is something wrong with them if they do.

"Courage," said Mark Twain is "resistance to fear, mastery of fear — not absence of fear." We walk forward along a path, fear is there, too. We keep walking.

To complete our dictionary drill, look up the word meaning the opposite of courage?

Many say cowardliness. Others say it is fear.

Although both of those answers could apply, I think the most appropriate answer is conformity. Courage is having the guts, nerve and heart to do things differently and allow progress to develop. Improvement does not happen by taking the path of least resistance and conforming to the way things have always been.

It takes leadership and courage to lead people through change and maintain focus, even when you have doubts about your own ability.

COURAGEOUS LEADERS IN THE BIBLE
In Gideon's battle with the Midianites,[1] Gideon probably felt secure about going into the battle with 32,000 soldiers. They had prepared, they were ready and I'm sure they were confident. With 32,000 soldiers they could overpower the opponent and give themselves credit for a victory, but God had other plans. *"Gideon, you have too many men—Israel may think they won with their own strength. Let the ones that want to leave, go."* Twenty-two thousand had no desire to stay. Ten thousand remained. God said, *"There are still too many, take*

them to the water and I will sift them out for you. " This time only 300 men were left to fight the battle.

Can you imagine how Gideon felt? When he had 32,000 soldiers it was easy to be a courageous leader – anyone could lead 32,000 to victory, but now he was to go into battle with only 300! Wow! That is a real test of courage and faith.

Gideon had to have complete faith in God. To build Gideon's courage, God allowed Gideon to slip into the enemy camp and overhear a conversation that confirmed God would deliver the camp to Gideon and his men. God provided the plan, and Gideon had the courage to carry it out against all odds.

Noah had the courage to follow God's plan, even though no one else believed the earth would be covered with water, and everyone thought Noah was crazy to build an ark.[2] Initially, Noah might have questioned, "You want me to build a what?" in response to God's instruction. But Noah also had courage – and the persistence to maintain obedience to God while being taunted, laughed at and scorned. That took an incredible amount of courage.

As a youth, David was full of courage and stood up for what he knew was right. He did not view Goliath as a giant, but rather as someone who mocked God – a stance that was not acceptable. David had the courage to trust God. *"The Lord who delivered me from the paw of the lion, and the paw of the bear will deliver me from the hand of this Philistine."*[3] When all of his associates were afraid to take a stand for God, he displayed total trust in God. He had the courage to do what was right, even though his peers discouraged him from trusting God completely.

Esther had been adopted by Mordecai, her older cousin, and raised by him after her parents died. Because of her beauty she was chosen by the king, a much older man with a track record for getting rid of women, to be his wife. Mordecai writes to her that the Jews are to be killed by the evil Haman and that she must help.

"What can I do?" she protested. "The king might put me to death."

"You must," Mordecai replied. "Perhaps this is the reason you became queen."

Then, something inside Esther changed. "Yes, I'll go to the king and plead for my people," she said, and then ordered Mordecai to get word to the other Jews to join her in a three-day fast.

When she goes to the king, if he doesn't hold out the golden scepter, Esther faces death. Imagine this young, 18-year-old girl dressed in a flowing gown, waiting outside the king's chambers. There is still time to change her mind. Instead, she goes forward and asks the king for mercy on her cousin Mordecai and the Jewish people. God knew exactly what He was and because He protected the Jews through Esther's courage, their numbers increased greatly, and many years later, the Son of God would emerge from their midst.

Barnabas had the courage to support Saul and let the disciples know that Saul had changed and had become a disciple of Jesus. Barnabas took Saul to the disciples and stood up for him when everyone else was afraid.[4] Without Barnabas' courage, Paul's ministry would have been much more difficult to begin.

Peter and John exhibited courage by standing up for Jesus even under the threat of the Sadducees. Even though they were put in jail, many who heard the message believed, and the number of

Jesus' followers grew. Peter and John had the courage to speak the truth.[5]

Paul had the courage to preach for Jesus. After his life radically changed, Paul shared the gospel soon after he had persecuted others for preaching the gospel. After Paul's conversion, people looked at him skeptically, and there was even a conspiracy to kill him. Paul still had the courage to accept his new role and lead thousands to Jesus.[6]

When Jesus was tempted in the desert, He had the courage to stand for what was right, even though he was tempted by his greatest needs. He made a choice that resisted Satan and kept his eyes on the long-range goal. His commitment was undeniable and unwavering.[7]

COURAGE TO PERSEVERE

When I began my business, success did not come easily or quickly. In fact, I was within weeks of giving up and returning to the corporate world when God provided a way for me to sustain, grow and prosper.

As I was pondering my next career move, I received a call from a business acquaintance, Mark Layton. I had known Mark during my time at FedEx but we were not particularly close – in fact, I had not seen him in years.

His call came at a time when I was financially broke – broke as a run over snake! He asked me to speak at a conference his company was sponsoring in Washington D.C. I agreed, thinking that this might be my last meeting representing CornerStone. Little did I know what God had in store.

After the conference, Mark and I had several meetings that resulted in me training all of Mark's managers worldwide – sustaining my business long enough to gather traction to move forward.

If I had created a list of 100 people whom I thought would be the people to have that kind of impact on my life and business, Mark Layton may not have made my list. However, he was #1 on God's list for me at that time and place in my life.

And, the story did not end there. Several weeks after I began working with Mark's team I received a call from a person named Kim in Phoenix. I had no idea who she was when I returned her call, but she said that I was the answer to her prayer of several years. Surprised by her comment, I asked why. She said that she was Mark Layton's sister and that she had been praying years for a Christian man to provide a positive influence for Mark, and I was that man.

God provided Mark for my business growth and me for Mark's spiritual growth – all at the same time, without either of us realizing it. Don't be surprised who God uses in your life at the right time and place if you have the courage to persevere.

Many people quit right before they cross the finish line. Your courage is ultimately measured by how much it takes to discourage you. Every leader is faced with this decision: "Do I continue, or is it best to let go of the dream?" The answer will be made clear only through consistent prayer for direction. If the answer is to stay the course, cling to the promise given in 2 Chronicles 20:17: *"Do not be afraid; do not be discouraged. Go out to face them tomorrow, and the Lord will be with you."* If the answer is to let go of the dream, have the courage to accept God's will for you.

ACTS OF COURAGE REQUIRED FOR
SUCCESSFUL LEADERSHIP

It takes courage to grow. The effective leader is never satisfied with the way things are, regardless of how great things may appear, and continually looks for ways to improve. The Bible says, *"Do not conform to the pattern of the world."*[8] Looking at things differently while improving the situation takes courage, wisdom, confidence and faith.

It takes courage to accept responsibility and to address issues that are preventing your team from being on track to accomplish your goals. Blaming mistakes on others does not take courage. In fact, placing blame is a cowardly act. It takes courage to accept outcomes without excuse and look to the future with optimism.

It takes courage to tell the truth while providing both positive and negative feedback to your boss. Telling the truth is not optional for the principle-based Christian leader. Regardless of how the feedback is accepted, it is your responsibility to give the feedback as you perceive it. The most effective way to give negative feedback is to communicate the situation and follow with a solution, as in "Now here is what we can do about it."

It takes courage to seek the truth. The higher your leadership position, the more difficult it becomes to find out the truth. Your courage, then, is accepting the truth and leading from that point – not from where you thought you were or where you think you should be. Facing reality is the key to improving a situation.

I once heard a story about a man who was elected president of a large company. At his congratulatory party, one of the older employees came to him and asked, "So, you are now the president?" "So it seems," the new president replied. The older employee said,

"Then you have heard the truth for the last time." It takes courage to seek the truth when others would rather please you by telling you what you want to hear.

It takes courage to have faith. The very definition of faith requires courage. Hebrews 11:1 tells us, *"Faith is evidence of things not seen."* Things not seen? That's the part that makes us uncomfortable. Do you have faith in the abilities of your people? Do you have faith in your product? Do you have faith in God's guidance? If you are in the Word, in prayer and listening to God's direction, then your only option is to have faith in God's direction.

It takes courage to reject the cynics. All organizations have people that sneer, joke about their leaders and never have solutions to problems. Some people protect themselves through cynicism. By expecting only the worst in people and things, they will not be disappointed. To be cynical requires no courage or faith. Cynicism doesn't solve issues or help build relationships or do anything but drain energy and emotions. Reject cynics by confronting them with facts and setting an example with optimism. If the cynics do not change, summon the courage to give them the opportunity to be cynical somewhere else.

It takes courage to speak out for what you believe, even though it might be controversial. The effective leader leaves no doubt as to where he stands. An old saying is, "We are proud to have our freedom to say what we believe anytime and anywhere. We just don't have the courage to do it." Most courageous acts are controversial – that's why they take courage.

It takes courage to persevere. There were times when Jesus was weary and struggled to complete His mission. His heart hurt so much that He cried. He was frustrated, mad, betrayed, needed rest and needed time to pray. When you feel like giving up on your mission, remember that He's felt that way himself … and He is with you now.

It takes courage to take risks. Risks worth taking are well thought out, are calculated and lead to an ultimate goal – and the result is worth the risk. Don't be afraid to take a risk. If you do not have some fear, it's not really a risk. The risks that are not worth taking are those that will not deliver the results you need to accomplish your goal, even if you are successful.

It takes courage to confront problems and responsibilities, especially if we have to admit a mistake or offer an apology. The principal quality that separates us from God is our human ego. The more you depend on God and humble yourself before Him, the easier it is to face issues, admit mistakes and apologize when you're wrong.

It takes courage to face criticism. Many leaders are paralyzed by the fear of being criticized. Most people, even strong-willed, self-confident leaders, desire to be liked and popular. The reality is that all leaders must make decisions that may be unpopular and subject to criticism. If you are leading people through change, you cannot expect every one to agree with you or see things your way.

It takes courage to realize your way might not be the only way to do what you are trying to accomplish. In fact, your way is probably one of hundreds of ways to attain the same goal. Display the courage and confidence to accept someone else's way, and be willing to try another approach.

COURAGE TO TRUST

It takes courage to look beyond the current situation into an area of hope and trust in God to provide for us. In Chuck Swindoll's terrific book, *Hope Again*,[9] he states, "Hope is a wonderful gift from God, a source of strength and courage in the face of life's harshest trials." God's gift of hope comes:

- When we are trapped in a tunnel of misery, hope points to the light at the end.

- When we are overworked and exhausted, hope gives us fresh energy.

- When we are discouraged, hope lifts our spirits.

- When we are tempted to quit, hope keeps us going.

- When we lose our way and confusion blurs the destination, hope dulls the edge of panic.

- When we struggle with a crippling disease or a lingering illness, hope helps us persevere beyond the pain.

- When we fear the worst, hope brings reminders that God is still in control.

- When we must endure the consequences of bad decisions, hope fuels our recovery.

- When we find ourselves unemployed, hope tells us we still have a future.

- When we are forced to sit back and wait, hope gives us the patience to trust.

- When we feel rejected and abandoned, hope reminds us we are not alone ... We'll make it.

- When we say our final farewell to someone we love, hope in the life beyond gets us through our grief.

The Bible promises that *"those who hope in the Lord will renew their strength. They will soar on wings like eagles: they will run and not grow weary, they will walk and not be faint."*[10] It takes courage to trust God's wonderful gift of hope.

COURAGE TO BE COMMITTED

Anytime your values conflict with the world's values, you will be criticized. Peter understood the courage required to carry the cross, saying, *"Dear friends, do not be surprised at the painful trial you are suffering, as though something strange were happening to you. But rejoice that you participate in the sufferings of Christ, so that you may be overjoyed when His glory is revealed. If you are insulted because of the name of Christ, you are blessed, for the Spirit of glory and of God rests on you."*[11] Paul also spoke of the courage required to carry the cross: *"For God did not give us a spirit of timidity, but a spirit of power, of love, and of self discipline. So don't be ashamed to testify about our Lord …"*[12]

We may suffer by following the biblical principles outlined in this book, but Peter instructed us to endure: *"So then those who suffer according to God's will should commit themselves to their faithful Creator and continue to do good."*[13]

I know of a man who agonized through a values clash but had the courage to choose to protect his integrity, regardless of the cost. This person, Don, was a man of faith and strong beliefs. He worked for an appraisal company in the Southwest. Don's job was to provide property appraisals based on recent sales in the area and based on his knowledge of the market. He was good at his job and enjoyed what he was doing.

When the real estate market was going through a slow period his boss pressured him to appraise high or low, depending on the situation. Don was to follow those directions or potentially lose his job. This is the real world – a conflict in values, a bad time to be looking for a job.

But, Don is a man of more courage, integrity and faith than most. He decided not to sacrifice his integrity. He refused to manipulate his appraisals, so he quit his job. He stepped out in faith and began his own appraisal company, even though his market timing could not have been much worse. Inflation was rampant, and the risk of starting a new business was high.

After struggling through the start-up, his business prospered. His company is now successful and is based on the values he would not sacrifice in his previous job. Don knew he really had no choice – he had chosen the values by which he would live his life. His courage was in living his commitment to himself and God.

Not every example of courage ends in a financial success story like Don's. In fact, many successful people have not been financially blessed. ***Ultimately, the true measurement of success is being able to look in the mirror and know that you had the courage to do what you felt was God's will for your life.***

The Bible teaches the ultimate reward for having such courage: *"So do not throw away your confidence; it will be richly rewarded. You need to persevere so that when you have done the will of God, you will receive what he has promised."*[14] It takes courage to commit to the will of God for your life and even more courage to act upon His will.

Moses had an unwavering commitment to do what was right, even though it was against his human nature. In the New Testament, Moses was described as a person who *"chose to be mistreated along with the people of God rather than to enjoy the pleasures of sin for a short time."*[15]

We have to make the same decision. Are the pleasures of sin worth my sacrifice of living for Christ? *A truly committed Christian does not have to weigh the consequences before making a decision. Because of his crystal clear values, the decision was made when he committed his all to Christ.*

SUMMARY

Experience the joy of having the courage to get the cross out of your pocket, lean your ladder on the building of God's principles and keep climbing. More than 20 times Jesus commanded, "Fear not."

It takes courage to trust Jesus when we are afraid, unsure and not confident in ourselves. I sincerely believe that the best God has for us is not far beyond what we fear the most.

Miguel de Cervantes once wrote, "He who loses wealth loses much; he who loses a friend loses more; but he who loses courage loses all."

You cannot be an effective leader by conforming to the method of least resistance. *Effective Christian leadership requires courage from the leader, trust from the follower, and direction from the Father.*

Do not pray for tasks equal to your powers.
Pray for powers equal to your tasks.
– Phillips Brooks

CHAPTER TWELVE

EXAMPLE

In everything set them an example by doing what is good.
— Titus 2:7

THE PRINCIPLE OF EXAMPLE

**Leadership results improve when
the leader becomes a positive role model.**

During the German occupation of his country in World War II, King Christian X of Denmark noticed the Nazi flag flying over a Danish public building. He immediately called the German commandant of the region, demanding the flag be taken down at once. The commandant refused.

"Then a soldier will go and take it down," said the king.

"He will be shot," threatened the commandant.

"I think not," replied the king, "for I shall be the soldier."

Within minutes the flag was taken down.

Whomever you are – king or civilian – whatever you do, you are a role model for everyone who sees you. The only choice you have is which role you will model. One of the most critical leadership responsibilities is to model the behavior you expect from others and what Christ expects from you.

ALEXANDER THE GREAT

Three hundred years ago, Alexander the Great led his troops across a hot and desolate plain. After 11 days of a grueling advance, he and his soldiers were near death from thirst. However, they pressed on.

At midday, two of his scouts brought Alexander what little water they had been able to find. It hardly filled a cup. His troops stood back and watched, expecting him to drink. Instead, he poured the water into the hot sand.

When questioned on his action, he said, "It's of no use for one to drink when many thirst." Alexander gave his followers all he had to give at that moment: example and inspiration.

PEOPLE FOLLOW PEOPLE

Your example of how you live communicates your values far more clearly than any words you may speak because: ***people follow people***. People do not follow speeches, memos, mission statements or state-of-the-business reports. You are making a difference – positive or not – at all times.

How do we learn from childhood and into maturity? By the observation of other people's behavior. The question is not, "Are people watching?" The question is, "What are the people seeing?" Whether you realize it or not, your example has a positive or negative influence not just on your team but on all the people they influence.

WHAT DOES THE BIBLE SAY?

After Jesus washed the feet of His disciples, He told them they should lead by example and what the results of their obedience would be. *"I have set you an example that you should do as I have done for you. I tell you the truth, no servant is greater than his master, nor is a messenger greater than the one who sent him. Now that you know these things, you will be blessed if you do them."*[1] These blessings will also be ours if we follow Jesus' example ... and how can we accomplish this in today's fast-paced world of business and commerce?

The answer is a simple one, particularly if you remember one of the first verses you learned from the Bible – The Golden Rule. We should treat others the way we would want them to treat us: *"So in everything, do to others what you would have them do to you."*[2]

Jesus spoke to the Pharisees about the negative influence they had on others: *"Woe to you experts in the law, because you have taken away the key to knowledge. You yourselves have not entered, and you have hindered those who were entering."*[3] Not only were the Pharisees making erroneous interpretations of law, but their example was keeping others away from the truth. At a different time, Jesus instructed the disciples to leave the Pharisees alone: *"Leave them; they are blind guides. If a blind man leads a blind man, both will fall in a pit."*[4] There are many people in leadership positions today who are blinded to the truths of biblically-based leadership.

James, the brother of Jesus, wrote, *"Who is wise and understanding among you? Let him show it by his good life, by deeds done in the humility that comes from wisdom."*[5] Your wisdom is illustrated by the example you set for others to follow.

Paul taught the Corinthians the true meaning of setting an example: *"I urge you to imitate me."*[6] Think about that! How much power and accountability would we have if we told everyone to imitate us?

Remember the survey mentioned in the first chapter? Only 14 percent of the leaders were seen as role models by their followers. How far off base are we from what Paul was teaching?

Titus was advised, *"In everything set an example by doing what is good. In your teaching show integrity, seriousness, and soundness of speech that cannot be condemned, so that those who oppose you may be ashamed because they have nothing bad to say about us."*[7]

Imagine your competitors being ashamed because they have nothing bad to say about you or your company?

Obviously, the Bible leaves no room for creative interpretations of leading by example. There are no exceptions when we are dealing with our bad bosses or for times when we are out of town and no one knows us. There are no exceptions when someone has hurt us, when we are angry, or when times are tough. There are no exceptions, period. Give no one reason to say anything bad about you!

ROLE MODELS

Recently, members of one church interviewed the administrators of elementary, middle and high schools surrounding the church. Each administrator was asked, "How can our church be of service to your school?"

The interviews were independent, and no one knew how any one else responded. Yet the answer was the same at every school: "Spend time with the kids, and provide them a role model for their future."

Our role as Christian leaders does not begin and end at work or in the church. Equally important is the influence we have in our neighborhoods.

Our workplace also needs positive role models – role models like Truett Cathy, the founder of Chick-fil-A, a committed Christian unwilling to sacrifice for the world.

In a highly competitive business (fast food), Cathy has made a stand. Chick-fil-A's restaurants are not open on Sundays.

Conventional wisdom says that is ridiculous because Sunday is a big day for fast food. Cathy's wisdom is his trust in God. For six days his employees work and on the seventh they rest. Any question about his values? Every Chick-fil-A store has a plaque engraved with this principle: "Associate yourselves only with those people you can be proud of – whether they work for you or you work for them."

Truett Cathy is leading by example!

WITNESSING AT WORK

Sometimes it is hard to evaluate the right time and place for witnessing. Non-believers at work are generally not interested in a prayer group or Bible study, but there are other methods to witness for Christ in the workplace. One way to effectively witness at work is to follow these four steps:

1. ***Prepare for the right time.*** Know what you believe. If you are unsure about your beliefs, it is doubtful that you will be able

to communicate a consistent message when the opportunity does occur. Study your Bible, know your beliefs and prepare for the time when God will provide you an opportunity to witness. The Bible says, *"Always be prepared to give an answer to everyone who asks you to give the reason for the hope that you have. But do this with gentleness and respect, keeping a clear conscience, so that those who speak maliciously against your good behavior in Christ may be ashamed of their slander."*[8]

2. **Pray for the non-believers and pray that the right time to witness will come along.** Pray consistently and earnestly for the salvation of each individual on your team and others, as well. Lift them up to God by name, and pray you or another believer will be given the opportunity to witness. Follow the attitude of Samuel: *"Far be it from me that I should sin against the Lord by failing to pray for you."*[9]

3. **Live what you believe.** Your greatest influence on non-believers is your behavior. If there is no difference between you and a non-believer, there is no reason for a non-believer to desire Christ. Stay in the Word and in prayer, and the difference will become obvious.

4. **Wait on God's time to witness.** The more you try to force your beliefs on someone, the more resistant they become. You control only your preparation, your prayers and your actions. Be consistent and dedicated in these three, and the time will come for you to share your faith.

EXAMPLE BY HUMILITY

Whatever your position – whether CEO or summer intern – the ability to show sincere humility is one of the most powerful examples you can set.

"But wait," you say. "Isn't humility contrary to a leader's personality? Isn't the nature of a leader to take charge and take pride in the results?"

But the humility to respect others' opinions, listen with empathy and seek the wisdom of your followers is an example that is biblically directed.

The Christian definition of humility is to be God-focused. It is impossible to be arrogant when you keep your focus on God!

The Book of Proverbs provides graphic descriptions of the results of pride and humility:

♦ *"When pride comes, then comes disgrace, but with humility comes wisdom."* (Proverbs 11:2)

♦ *"Pride only brings quarrels, but wisdom is found in those who take advice."* (Proverbs 13:10)

♦ *"The fear of the Lord teaches a man wisdom, and humility comes before honor."* (Proverbs 15:33)

♦ *"An arrogant man stirs up strife, but he who trusts in the Lord will prosper."* (Proverbs 18:25)

♦ *"Pride goes before destruction, a haughty spirit before a fall."* (Proverbs 16:18)

The New Testament is just as clear about humility:

♦ *"For everyone who exalts himself will be humbled, and he who humbles himself will be exalted."* (Luke 14:11)

♦ *"Do not think of yourself more highly than you ought, but rather think of yourself with sober judgment, in accordance with the measure of faith God has given you."* (Romans 12:3)

♦ *"Do nothing out of selfish ambition or vain conceit, but in humility consider others better than yourselves. Each of you should look not only to your own interests, but also to the interests of others."* (Philippians 2:3-4)

Pride = disgrace, quarrels and destruction.
Humility = wisdom, honor and exaltation.

Jesus is our example of ultimate humility. *"And being found in appearance as a man, he humbled himself and became obedient to death – even death on a cross!"*

The cultivation of humility is essential for the Christian leader, because humility is not often found among non-Christians. Humility is opposed to our nature but is in keeping with Jesus Christ's example.

LEADING BY EXAMPLE

If your goal is becoming a positive example in every step of your walk, you may want to use some of these tools:

1. Always treat others the way they would want to be treated.

2. Be available to anyone who needs your help.

3. Praise in public, criticize in private, and surround your criticism with praise.

4. Never criticize an employee for making a customer happy.

5. Know what you can and cannot change, and act accordingly.

6. Be predictable – do what you say you will do.

7. Be unpredictable in trying new things and motivating people to achieve results.

8. Walk your talk.

9. Admit when you are wrong and apologize.

10. Learn how to say "no" to avoid overcommitting.

11. Be an active listener and take action on what you hear.

12. Help others on the way up the corporate ladder.

13. Trust your employees, or find employees that you can trust.

14. Get feedback from all levels of employees and customers.

15. Treat everyone fairly and consistently.

16. Develop your staff into a team and never pit them against each other.

17. Smile. It is contagious.

18. Continually look for improvements and fight complacency in your professional, personal, and spiritual life.

19. Embrace change and become a change master.

20. Cultivate family relationships.

SUMMARY

You have no choice. Leadership demands you serve as a role model for your followers. So, what's the difference between Christian and non-Christian leaders?

For starters, the principle-based leader does not ignore or take advantage of that responsibility. With Jesus as the ultimate example, Christian leaders are committed to be humble, to treat everyone with dignity and respect, and to be compassionate.

Christian leaders are to address their followers' needs, to remain close to their followers and to be servants. "... *The fruit of the spirit is love, joy, peace, patience, kindness, goodness, faithfulness, gentleness and self control.*"[10]

Your every action is an example to others. You always lead, and everything counts!

"Example is not the main thing in influencing others.
It is the only thing."
— Albert Schweitzer

CHAPTER THIRTEEN

PREPARATION

It is more blessed to give than to receive.
— Acts 20:35

THE PRINCIPLE OF PREPARATION

Leadership results improve to the extent to which the leader develops himself and his team.

What did you do to prepare to get to where you are right now?

Each Friday evening before bedtime during soccer season, a six-year-old boy lays out his soccer cleats, his socks, soccer shorts and soccer jersey next to his bed just before being tucked in. It is almost as if he expects to arise the next day, magically fly into the carefully sequenced pieces of his uniform and report to the nearby soccer field. In his own small way, he is preparing to do his best at the soccer game Saturday morning.

The greatest leaders are those who also prepare themselves by continuing to learn and improve every day. Leaders who choose to rest on their knowledge – those who are not committed to personal improvement – are doomed to fail. It's that simple ... there's no other way to put it. **Complacency is the root of mediocrity.**

In Ephesians, Paul gave counsel to the church on preparing for the challenges of the future. His direction was to know their resources: *"Be strong in the Lord, and put on the full armor of God."*[1]

Let me set the stage: Paul was in the midst of trials that we can only imagine. He was in prison – in solitary confinement – and chained to an armed guard 24 hours a day. History tells us that he was most likely chained wrist-to-wrist and ankle-to-ankle. The guards were on duty for approximately six hours each shift. As Paul was writing those words, he was no doubt preaching to the guards as he described the armor of the guard chained right beside him.

The armor Paul described for the Christians to equip themselves in preparation for the day of evil included the following:

- ♦ The **Belt** represents the truth to defend against the lies of Satan.

- ♦ The **Breastplate** represents God's righteousness that protects our hearts and ensures God's approval.

- ♦ The **Footgear** represents our readiness to spread the gospel.

- ♦ The **Shield** represents our faith, which protects us from Satan's arrows.

♦ The **Helmet** represents our salvation that protects our minds from doubting God's work.

♦ The **Sword** represents the word of God to use against Satan.

Each piece of God's armor protects us and prepares us for the battles we will face. But what about protection for the backside of the soldier?

As long as the soldiers are moving forward, they are protected. If they are running from the opposition, they are unprotected, and any missing piece leaves us vulnerable to the opposition.

Are you prepared?

Whatever our path in business, we will always be faced with difficult choices, choices that may not clearly be right or wrong, or choices that challenge our faith, commitment and desire to keep going.

The key to making your best decisions is to precisely understand your values. What is the most important thing – the one thing – that cannot be compromised under any circumstance? Until you know your number one value, you cannot commit to your number two, three or four values. Once your values are identified, your choices are easier to make.

PREPARING FOR PERSONAL DEVELOPMENT

As Paul described to his Christian compatriots, preparation is critical if we are to be strong in our commitments and consistent in our walk through our future challenges. The following 11 tips will help you prepare:

1. *Make sure your job is congruent with your values.* Recent surveys tell us up to 80 percent of all working Americans

occupy jobs that are wrong for them. They say they are discontented because of a conflict in their values and a conflict with God's will for their lives! *If any area of your job conflicts with your value system and what God wants you to do, you are guaranteed to be miserable, and your employees will be miserable as well.*

We all know extremely intelligent, successful, unhappy people who are facing this clash of values. Maybe their job requires constant time away from their family. The money is great, but their families mean so much more.

These people will never reach their potential until their values align with their actions. Ecclesiastes 5:19-20 says a person should: *"accept his lot and be happy in his work – this is a gift of God. He seldom reflects on the days of his life, because God keeps him occupied with gladness of heart."*

You cannot be happy at work if you are continually experiencing a clash with your values.

"In order to succeed," the late Will Rogers said, "you must know what you are doing, like what you are doing and believe in what you are doing."

Are you succeeding? Check to see if the answers to these four questions align with your values:

a. *How do you feel about your job?* Are you proud of the job you have chosen to do? Do you enjoy telling people what you do? How do you feel about your chosen profession? A passion for your job will create energy and focus for you to lead others. If you are not comfortable sharing with others what you do, you are likely in the wrong job.

b. *How do you feel about the activities your job requires?* Is the travel too much? Do you have to sacrifice your integrity? Do you enjoy the daily activities? Do you look forward to going to work? Are the activities aligned with your values? You spend at least eight hours a day at work … if you spend that time doing things that conflict with your value system you are guaranteed misery.

c. *How do you view your ability to do the job well?* Do you think this is God's direction for your life? Do you feel you can excel at this job? Do you enjoy the challenges to your ability that this job provides? Are you working in your area of excellence? Do you believe in yourself enough to lead others to the unknown? Your confidence in being the best in your chosen profession is a major influence on your success.

d. *How do you feel about the company you work for?* Do the company values align with your personal values? Are you proud of the product or services you represent? Do you enjoy the people you work for and with? Do you believe your product is a good deal for your customer? If you answered no to any of those questions, begin searching for a company where you can feel good about going to work.

You cannot achieve long-term happiness in any job where the corporate culture values clash with God's direction for you, your work and your life.

2. ***Live a balanced life and have a feedback system for knowing when you lose your balance.*** The way to maintain balance is to have goals for each of the five major areas in your life: professional, personal, physical, spiritual and emotional. Create an upper control limit (the most time you will spend

in this area) and a lower control limit (the least amount of time required to fulfill your goals), and stay within your boundaries. Establish goals to prevent you from ignoring one important area because you are too focused on another area. Stay within your boundaries.

Balancing your goals isn't always easy. The first step is to identify each of your roles and write them down. Then establish a monthly goal for each role and the actions necessary to accomplish that goal. Do this for two months and you will see a difference in your satisfaction at work and at home.

3. *Read the Bible, pray and read something positive every day.* Find a consistent time and place to read your Bible. The Bible and your prayer life are the principal means through which God provides direction. Romans 15:4 tells us that the Bible is our encouragement: *"For everything that was written in the past was written to teach us, so that through endurance and the encouragement of the scriptures we might have hope."* None of our problems are new or unique to us. The Bible teaches solutions to each one. *"Your word is a lamp to my feet and a light for my path."*[2] Keep the light on by having your Bible open!

Pray daily. Practice until you are in consistent prayer communication with God. *"Cast all of your anxiety on Him because He cares for you."*[3] Jesus gave us the example: *"Very early in the morning, while it was still dark, Jesus got up, left the house and went off to a solitary place, where he prayed."*[4] Jesus prayed for himself, His followers and all the people touched by His followers. That is a great blueprint of prayer for all leaders. James 5:16 tells us that the *"prayer of a righteous man is powerful and effective."* Find the time to dedicate yourself to prayer.

Read about your profession and new skills. There are hundreds of books to help you become more satisfied and productive in your chosen profession, yet most people do not read one book a year. Unfortunately, with the pace of today's business and the exponential increases in information and technology, continuing education is no longer an option for success. It is a necessity! Think about it this way: A Ph.D. degree earned today may be obsolete within five years of graduation because information and theories are changing so rapidly.

Whatever role you have chosen, make the choice to be the best in that profession. By spending about 10 minutes a day reading, you can finish a book in a month and join the top one percent in the nation in your chosen profession.

School is never out for the Christian professional. The more you learn, the greater your chances for a prosperous and satisfying career.

4. **Listen to CD's.** The average person spends more than 500 hours per year in his car – the equivalent of twelve 40-hour weeks. Convert half of that time into a learning experience and in doing so, create more time for your and your family. CD's are available to educate and motivate you in your spiritual, professional and personal life. The more productive you are during your "drive time," the better prepared you will be to face the challenges of the day.

5. **Invest in your growth.** The return on your investment is self-esteem and job satisfaction. In Colossians 3:23 we are directed, *"Whatever you do, work at it with all your heart, as working for the Lord, not for men."* The disciples knew how important it was

to keep learning. They learned by experiencing God's wonders.
They learned by asking Jesus to keep teaching them.

6. ***Develop an accountability group.*** Pick one or two ambitious
people that you admire who are positive and fun. Meet with
them once a week – just to talk. This is a good accountability
system for you and will help you keep your sanity when you
need to just talk things out. In Hebrews 10:25, Paul said, *"Let
us not give up meeting together, as some are in the habit of doing, but
let us encourage one another – and all the more as you see the day
approaching."* Paul also taught the Roman church that *"I long
to see you so that I may impart to you some spiritual gift to make
you strong – that is, that you and I may be mutually encouraged by
each other's faith."*[5] Having a group to whom you can relate
and be yourself with is important. Pick a group, find the
time, choose the place and lift each other's spirits.

7. ***Teach what you know to others.*** You become what you teach.
Be a consistent communicator of what you desire to become,
and that will be the standard you live. Jesus' last words of
instruction were clear: *"Go and make disciples ... and teach
them to obey everything I have commanded you."*[6] When you
teach, you not only follow God's direction but you also create
built-in accountability for you in His work.

8. ***Create your own personal goals and mission.*** Someone without
purpose and goals is crippled. You cannot fulfill any dream
without first understanding your purpose. It has been said
that less than five percent of people have personal goals they
are actually working to accomplish. Your personal goals are
the rudder for your life; they steer you in the right direction.
You will not achieve your purpose without accurately defining
what you are trying to accomplish.

Check out yourself by completing this list of your commitments in the five major areas of your life and set goals for your improvement.

PERSONAL LEVELS OF COMMITMENT

1= Not Committed 2 = Committed When Popular
3 = Lukewarm Committed 4 = Committed When Convenient
5 = Totally Committed

◆ My commitment to Jesus Christ _____

My actions to increase my commitment: _____

_____

_____

_____

◆ My commitment to my family _____

My actions to increase my commitment: _____

_____

_____

_____

◆ My commitment to my team at work _____

My actions to increase my commitment: _____

_____

_____

_____

♦ My commitment to my health   _____

My actions to increase my commitment:_____

_____

_____

_____

♦ My commitment to use my talents to help others   _____

My actions to increase my commitment:_____

_____

_____

_____

The better you define where you are currently, and where you want to be, the more committed you become to their accomplishment. After you have defined, written down and committed to your actions, involve others by sharing what you are trying to accomplish. People that you care about, trust, respect and mentor all want to help you achieve your dreams. Let them know your goals so they can encourage you and celebrate with you as you accomplish them.

9. **Keep yourself physically healthy.** Jesus taught his disciples the value of physical renewal. When the disciples told Jesus what they had been doing in their ministry, they said they had not even had time to eat. Jesus directed them to *"come with me to a quiet place and get some rest."*[7] We all need vacations to escape the pressures of our daily work. Take time for renewal. Your ability to accept control of the elements of your life that are controllable is key to your physical and mental health.

10. ***Keep your sense of humor.*** When you stop laughing at yourself, you are taking yourself too seriously. We are all different; we are all unique. Enjoy the differences in personalities within your workgroup. The Bible says, *"A cheerful heart is good medicine, but a crushed spirit dries up the bones."*[8]

A good sense of humor is a requirement for job satisfaction. The Bible says to *"not think of ourselves more highly than we should."*[9] People who can laugh at life and enjoy the world around them are healthier and happier. Use your sense of humor to make life fun!

11. ***Keep your faith.*** Even the disciples who saw Jesus perform miracles firsthand lost their faith. Think of some of the astonishing things they witnessed:

- Five thousand people fed with five loaves and two fish[10]

- Jesus' command over the winds and sea[11]

- Demons transferred from a man into pigs[12]

- The sick healed[13]

- The paralyzed made to walk[14]

- Lepers healed[15]

- Jesus walking on water[16]

- Blind men gaining sight[17]

- Mute men beginning to speak[18]

- Dead men coming back to life[19]

- Water turned to wine[20]

♦ A man's ear restored[21]

♦ A lame man healed[22]

After seeing Jesus perform many of these miracles, you would think their faith would never waver. However, the 12 men who were closest to Jesus still had little faith. No wonder we have to work so hard at growing in our faith. I know how difficult it is to have the faith to keep going when things are tough. I have seen God provide for me when only His divine intervention could explain why certain things happened. Yet when times are tough, I tend to lose faith in the One who has always provided. The only way I know to grow my faith is to grow spiritually through the Word and prayer and let God provide in His way with His timing. The Bible says, *"Without faith it is impossible to please God."*[23]

DOES GOD HEAR US?

We must possess the faith to know that God is listening to our prayers. Sometimes we lose our patience while waiting on God's answers. Dr. John Bisagno of First Baptist Church, Houston, Texas, preached a sermon on how God answers prayers that have been an inspiration to me for more than twenty years. According to Dr. Bisagno, God answers prayer in one of four ways:

♦ *Slow.* The timing is not right. You may have prepared all of your life for the opportunity and you are ready, but the timing is not right for you from God's perspective. Be still and wait on the Lord. *"There is a time for everything, and a season for every activity under heaven."*[24] Keep yourself prepared for when the timing is right.

♦ *Grow.* The timing is right, the job is available, but you are not right. You need to grow before the situation is right for you.

Commit yourself to the improvement needed for the next opportunity. *"Show me your ways, O Lord, teach me your paths, guide me in your truth and teach me, for you are my God and my Saviour, and my hope is in you all day long."*[25] Keep growing until God opens the right door for you.

♦ **No.** You – and the timing – are not right. Too many times we try to fit a round peg into a square hole. The timing is not right, and we are not right, so we should pick up and move on. *"Blessed is the man who finds wisdom, the man who gains understanding."*[26] Understand that even if the situation appears fantastic, if you are not right and the timing is not right, the worst result you could experience is to get what you were praying for.

♦ **Go.** When you and the timing are right, you'll know it. How? You'll have peace. You'll look forward with optimism. No one has to tell you this opportunity is the right one – you know it! Thank God and enjoy! *"Then I heard the voice of the Lord saying, 'Whom shall I send? And who will go for us?' And I said, 'Here am I. Send me!'"*[27] Be ready to go when you and the timing are right!

So, what happens when prayer is not answered? What happens when we feel our faith and trust and God ebbing away. Without a doubt, there are some who give up too soon … just before they turn the corner to success.

Successful people keep moving even when they are scared and have made mistakes … unsuccessful people quit before they have a chance to be successful.

The following story illustrates what happens to many on the road to success:

A man meets a guru in the road. The man asks the guru, "Which way is success?"

The bearded sage doesn't speak, but points to a place in the distance.

The man, thrilled by the prospect of quick and easy success, rushes off. Suddenly, there comes a loud "splat." Eventually, the man now tattered and stunned, limps back, assuming he must have taken a wrong turn; so he repeats his question to the guru, who again points silently in the same direction.

The man obediently walks off, and this time the splat sound is deafening. When the man crawls back he is bloody, broken and irate. "I asked you which way to success," he screams at the guru. "I followed your direction, and all I got was splatted! No more of this pointing! Talk!"

Only then does the guru speak, and says: "Success is that way. Just a little past splat."

How many of us are strong enough and have enough faith to make the effort long enough to get past splat? Never give up! Run the race!

The essence of temptation is to stop running as soon as you hit splat. Hebrews 12:1, *"... let us throw off everything that hinders and the sin that so easily entangles, and let us run with perseverance the race marked out for us."*

Keep your faith in God and the direction He has for your life.

"If you employed study, thinking and planning time daily, you could develop and use the power that can change the course of your destiny."
— W. Clement Stone

THE ULTIMATE VICTORY

Leap for joy, because great is your reward in heaven.
– Luke 6:23

L eadership can't be bought nor inherited. It cannot be given to you as a present. It cannot be stolen from someone else that has it. It cannot be accepted when you are promoted.

Leadership is earned!

♦ By living the principles taught in the Bible and expressed in this book

♦ By maintaining your integrity even when it hurts

♦ By accepting responsibility for all you control

♦ By surrounding yourself with committed people

♦ By creating a guiding vision for others to follow

- By communicating with crystal clear clarity

- By overcoming adversity that comes our way

- By being optimistic and looking for the best in others

- By empowering others to do what they do best

- By making positive changes

- By having the courage to do what's right

- By leading by your example

- By preparing yourself and your people for the future

Whatever you do, wherever you are and wherever you go, you are a leader – with influence far greater than you will ever be able to comprehend.

The average person comes in contact with thousands of people in his or her lifetime. You influence some of those people even when you are not aware that anyone is watching. *You affect others and you do make a difference!*

Think of the people who have made a difference in your life:

Remember that Sunday School teacher who influenced your life? She sacrificed her time and talent to take the time to teach you. Hundreds of kids participated in her class over the years, and the teacher probably had no idea the positive impression she made on you. Her impact was never measured by any plaques or awards, but her impact is measured every day in the way you live your life.

Remember the schoolteacher you wanted to imitate? That teacher probably never heard about the positive difference he/she made in you and the way he/she helped change your life. There was no test to take or report to measure those changes.

Remember the pastor who was so eloquent in the pulpit, yet took the time to get to know you personally? His words and his actions shaped your life, yet there is no report at the church that measured his impact.

Remember the secretary who led the Bible study at work on Thursday mornings and consistently prayed for the business and the people in the company? Remember how she ministered and soothed the pain when fellow employees were going through hardships that could not be explained? There is no annual recognition banquet for her or those like her and the influence she had on the lives of others.

The traditional ways we measure success and effectiveness do not measure long-term impact. The Sunday School teacher's effectiveness might have been measured by attendance each Sunday. The schoolteacher's effectiveness might have been measured by achievement test scores at the end of the year. The Bible study leader might have been measured at work by how quickly and accurately reports were distributed. The pastor's effectiveness might have been measured by church growth, but none of those important people were measured by the impact they had on your life.

If they had been only concerned with attendance, grades, reports and church growth, they would not have cared about the difference they had made in the lives of others. Fortunately, they did care. They looked beyond the normal measurements and rewards and then went out of their way to positively impact your life.

Similarly, leadership success cannot be measured by the corporate bottom line alone. Although profitability is important, your ultimate victory will come in rewards far beyond what you can imagine.

Set your leadership goals and pay the price to accomplish them, but remember that **the ultimate success of the Christian leader will not be measured by any report, plaque, banquet or trophy here on earth.**

But before you go away from this book too narrowly focused, you'll need to answer these questions: What good is success if you lose your family? What good is success if there is no room in your life for a relationship with Christ?

"For no one can lay any foundation other than the one already laid, which is Jesus Christ. If any man builds on this foundation using gold, silver, costly stones, wood, hay, or straw, his work will be shown for what it is."[1]

"If you judge success solely by your possessions, you are measuring against what the Bible says is meaningless: *"Whoever loves money never has money enough; whoever loves wealth is never satisfied with his income. This too is meaningless."*[2]

Don't get me wrong. Money does not destroy people. There are many Christians who are blessed financially and are living in God's will. In fact, 1 Timothy 5:8 clearly expresses the importance of providing for our families: *"If anyone does not provide for his relatives, and especially for his immediate family, he has denied the faith and is worse than an unbeliever."* However, Jesus talked about money in His parables more than any other subject. Sixteen of Christ's thirty-eight parables dealt with money. Christ knew the temptations that come with money. My point is that measuring a man's success just by his financial portfolio is a false and temporary measurement. Paul instructed Timothy to teach those that are rich to *"not be arrogant or put their hope in wealth, which is so uncertain, but put their hope in God, who richly provides us everything for our enjoyment."*[3]

There is no success without Christ! *"It is required that those who have been given a trust must prove faithful … it is the Lord who judges me … He will bring to light what is hidden in darkness and will expose the motives of men's hearts. At that time each will receive his praise from God."*[4] In Ecclesiastes, Solomon wrote about enjoying life while understanding our purpose in life. His conclusion was, *"Fear God and keep his commandments, for this is the whole duty of man. For God will bring every deed into judgment, including every hidden thing, whether it is good or evil."*[5] Our success comes in bringing glory to God.

My final note is to remind you of the ultimate non-negotiable of life — your decision to be a follower of Jesus Christ and a leader in bringing others to Christ is the most important decision you will ever make. As Jesus said, *"By their fruit you will recognize them."*[6] Our fruit is displayed by applying what we know and having others see Jesus in us wherever we are.

Rudyard Kipling wrote a poem describing what would happen if all Christians leave their crosses in their pockets and lean their ladders on the wrong buildings:

> They shut the road through the woods
> Seventy years ago.
> Weather and rain have undone it again
> And now you would never know
> There once was a road through the woods.
> — Rudyard Kipling

David spoke of the shortness of our lives in Psalms: *"As for man, his days are like grass, he flourishes like a flower of the field; and the wind blows over it and it is gone, and its place remembers it no more."*[7] The Christian influence on society will be washed out like an eroded road and blown away like a flower in the field unless Christians replace the liberal teachings of television and the media with biblically-based leadership.

Our goal should be as Paul wrote at the end of his productive and fulfilled life: *"I have fought the good fight, I have finished the course, I have kept the faith."* (2 Timothy 4:7). What a fabulous epitaph! He seized every moment and passionately pursued God's will for his life. No remorse, no regrets!

If we Christian leaders take the crosses out of our pockets and lean our ladders on God's building, our children will grow in Godly homes, our students will live by Christian values, our business associates will see integrity, our churches will experience committed followers and everyone will see Jesus in us. That is what really counts!

Our ultimate victory will come when we are face-to-face with the Father and He tells us, **"Well done, thy good and faithful servant."**

I can't wait!

May the God of Peace, who through the blood of the eternal covenant brought back from the dead our Lord Jesus, that great shepherd of the sheep, equip you with everything good for doing his will, and may he work in us what is pleasing to him through Jesus Christ, to whom be glory for ever and ever. Amen.
Hebrews 13:20

APPENDIX

THE PRINCIPLES OF SUCCESSFUL LEADERSHIP

PRINCIPLE #1: THE PRINCIPLE OF INTEGRITY

My lips shall not speak wickedness, nor my tongue utter deceit.
– Job 27:4

Leadership results improve in proportion to the level of trust earned by the leader.

PRINCIPLE #2: THE PRINCIPLE OF RESPONSIBILITY

From everyone who has been given much, much will be demanded; and from the one who has been entrusted with much, much more will be asked.
– Luke 12:48

Leadership results improve dramatically when the leader and his team accept total responsibility for their actions.

PRINCIPLE #3: THE PRINCIPLE OF COMMITMENT

Whoever wants to be great among you must be your servant, and whoever wants to be greatest of all must be the slave of all.
– Mark 10:43-44 (LB)

Leadership results improve to the extent that the leader respects, recognizes, and develops his or her team.

PRINCIPLE #4: THE PRINCIPLE OF VISION

Where there is no vision, the people perish.
– Proverbs 29:18 (KJV)

Leadership results improve when leaders communicate a crystal clear vision and a convincing reason for accomplishing the vision.

PRINCIPLE #5: THE PRINCIPLE OF COMMUNICATION

Do not let any unwholesome talk come out of your mouths, but only what is helpful for building others up according to their areas, that it may benefit those who listen.

– Ephesians 4:29

Leadership results improve when followers understand their role and are rewarded for their accomplishments.

PRINCIPLE #6: THE PRINCIPLE OF ADVERSITY

Consider it pure joy, my brothers, whenever you face trials of many kinds, because you know that the testing of your faith develops perseverance.

– James 1:2-3

Leadership results improve to the extent that the leader is able to overcome adversity.

PRINCIPLE #7: THE PRINCIPLE OF OPTIMISM

Whatever things are true, whatsoever things are honest, whatsoever things are just, whatsoever things are lovely, whatsoever things are of good report, if there be any virtue, and if there be any peace, think on these things.

– Philippians 4:8

Leadership results improve in direct proportion to the self-concept and optimism of the leader.

PRINCIPLE #8: THE PRINCIPLE OF OPTIMISM

So they shook their feet in protest against them and went to Iconium. And the disciples were filled with joy and with the Holy Spirit.

– Acts 13:51-52

Leadership results improve to the extent that the leader is able to embrace change and accept responsibility for change.

PRINCIPLE #9: THE PRINCIPLE OF EMPOWERMENT

Give and it shall be given to you; good measure, pressed down, and shaken together, and running over, shall men give into your bosom.

— Luke 6:38 (KJV)

Leadership results improve as your team is provided the opportunity to accept total ownership of their work.

PRINCIPLE #10: THE PRINCIPLE OF COURAGE

And be not conformed to this world; but be ye transformed by the renewing of your mind, that ye may prove what is that good, and acceptable, and perfect, will of God.

— Romans 12:2 (KJV)

Leadership results improve in proportion to the leader's courage to address issues affecting his team.

PRINCIPLE #11: THE PRINCIPLE OF EXAMPLE

In everything set them an example while doing what is good.

— Titus 2:7

Leadership results improve when the leader is a positive role model.

PRINCIPLE #12: THE PRINCIPLE OF PREPARATION

It is more blessed to give than to receive.

— Acts 20:35

Leadership results improve to the extent to which the leader develops himself and his team.

INSPIRATIONAL PASSAGES FOR LEADERS CARRYING THE CROSS

These passages are the author's favorites for keeping his eyes on the cross.

James 1:12 — *Blessed is the man who perseveres under trial, because when he has stood the test, he will receive the crown of life that God has promised to those that love Him.*

Psalms 27:14 — *Wait on the Lord: be of good courage, and He shall strengthen thine heart.*

Isaiah 42:16 — *I will lead the blind by ways they have not known, along unfamiliar paths I will guide them; I will turn the darkness into light before them and make the rough places smooth. These things I will do; I will not forsake them.*

1 Peter 4:16 — *If you suffer as a Christian, do not be ashamed, but praise God that you bear His name.*

Philippians 4:10 — *I have learned to be content whatever the circumstances.*

Philippians 4:13 — *I can do everything through Him who gives me strength.*

Philippians 4:19 — *And my God will meet all of your needs according to His glorious riches in Christ Jesus.*

Hebrews 10:36   *You need to persevere so that when you have done the will of God, you will receive what He has promised.*

1 Timothy 6:17   *Command those who are rich in his present world not to be arrogant nor to put their hope in wealth, which is so uncertain, but to put their hope in God, who richly provides us with everything for our enjoyment.*

Proverbs 3:5-6   *Trust in the Lord with all your heart and lean not on your own understanding; in all your ways acknowledge Him, and He will make your paths straight.*

Joshua 1:9   *Have I not commanded you? Be strong and courageous. Do not be terrified, do not be discouraged, for the Lord your God will be with you wherever you go.*

Psalm 127:1 (KJV)   *Except the Lord build the house, they labor in vain that build it.*

1 Corinthians 10:13   *No temptation has seized you except what is common to man. And God is faithful; He will not let you be tempted beyond what you can bear. But when you are tempted, He will also provide a way out so that you can stand up under it.*

1 Corinthians 9:24   *Do you know that in a race all the runners run, but only one gets the prize? Run in such a way as to get the prize.*

Galatians 6:8-9   *The one who sows to please his sinful nature, from that nature will reap destruction; the one who sows to please the Spirit, from the Spirit will reap eternal life. Let us not become weary in doing good, for at the proper time we will reap a harvest if we do not give up.*

Philippians 3:13-14   *But one thing I do! Forgetting what is behind and straining toward what is ahead, I press on toward the goal to win the prize for which God has called me heavenward in Christ Jesus.*

2 Timothy 1:12   *That is why I am suffering as I am. Yet, I am not ashamed, because I know whom I have believed, and am convinced that He is able to guard what I have entrusted to Him for that day.*

Psalm 56:3   *When I am afraid, I will trust in you.*

1 Corinthians 16:13   *Be on your guard; stand firm in the faith; be men of courage; be strong. Do everything in love.*

Isaiah 40:31   *But those who hope in the Lord will renew their strength. They will soar on wings like eagles, they will run and not grow weary, they will walk and not faint.*

Psalm 46:1   *God is our refuge and strength, an ever present help in trouble.*

2 Chronicles 26:5   *As long as he sought the Lord, God gave him success.*

Isaiah 54:10

Though the mountains be shaken and the hills be removed, yet my unfailing love for you will not be shaken nor my covenant of peace be removed, says the Lord, who has compassion on you.

2 Timothy 2:15

Do your best to present yourself to God as one approved, a workman who does not need to be ashamed and who correctly handles the word of truth.

Romans 15:13

May the God of hope fill you with all joy and peace as you trust in Him, so that you may overflow with hope by the power of the Holy Spirit.

John 14:27

Peace I leave with you; my peace I give you. I do not give to you as the world gives. Do not let your hearts be troubled and do not be afraid.

REFERENCES

INTRODUCTION – JACUZZIS, LEADERS AND THE CROSS
[1] 1 Corinthians 3:19
[2] Ephesians 2:10

CHAPTER ONE – THE CALL FOR LEADERSHIP
[1] Exodus 3-4
[2] Robert Kelley, *The Power of Followership* (Doubleday, 1992)
[3] Ibid.
[4] Shipper and Wilson Study, 1996
[5] Ibid.
[6] Ibid.
[7] Robert Kelley, *The Power of Followership* (Doubleday, 1992)
[8] Frederick Reichheld, *The Loyalty Effect* (Harvard Business Press, 1996)
[9] Exodus 3:11-4:17
[10] Exodus 4:29-31
[11] Ecclesiastes 11:4

CHAPTER TWO – INTEGRITY
[1] John C. Maxwell, *Developing the Leader Within You* (Nelson, 1993)
[2] Genesis 43:12
[3] Book of Job
[4] Romans 12:21
[5] "Disabled by a Paper Cut," *Readers' Digest*, November 1997
[6] Romans 7:18-19
[7] James 1:12
[8] Titus 2:7-8
[9] 1 Peter 3:14

CHAPTER THREE – RESPONSIBILITY
[1] Hebrews 4:13
[2] Matthew 25:14-30
[3] James 3:1
[4] David Hartley-Leonard, "Perspectives," *Newsweek*, August 24, 1987
[5] Stephen Covey, *Seven Habits of Highly Effective People* (Simon & Schuster, 1990)

Chapter Four – Commitment
1 Matthew 9:36
2 Matthew 15:29-39
3 Matthew 13:34
4 Revelation 3:15
5 1 Corinthians 12:24-31
6 John 13:12-17
7 Luke 14:11
8 Mark 12:30
9 Eugene Habecker, *Leading With A Follower's Heart* (Victor, 1990)
10 1 John 2:15
11 2 Timothy 3:12
12 Luke 12:34
13 Luke 22:42
14 Galatians 6:2
15 Mark 8:38

Chapter Five – Vision
1 Genesis 12:1-3
2 Exodus 3:10
3 Joshua 1:6-3:5
4 Matthew 6:22-23
5 Matthew 4:19-20
6 Luke 4:18
7 Quoted in Stephen B. Oates, *Let The Trumpet Sound: The Life of Martin Luther King, Jr.* (Harper and Row, 1982)
8 John C. Maxwell, *Developing The Leader Within You* (Nelson, 1993)

Chapter Six – Communications
1 Exodus 3:1-3
2 Luke 9:23-24
3 Luke 3:22
4 Luke 19:17
5 Richard Hussman and John Hatfield, *Managing The Equity Factor,* (Houghton Mifflin, 1987)
6 Mark 4:38
7 Luke 10:40
8 Mark 10:35-45
9 Acts 26:16-18

[10] Mark 13:4-23
[11] Matthew 28:19-20
[12] Luke 10:40-42
[13] Luke 18:1
[14] Psalm 46:10
[15] Isaiah 30:15
[16] 1 Thessalonians 5:19
[17] Luke 18:41

CHAPTER SEVEN – ADVERSITY
[1] Proverbs 27:12 (LB)
[2] Proverbs 18:13-17
[3] Mark 4:35-41
[4] Genesis 4:1-10
[5] Mark 3:25
[6] Proverbs 23:23 (LB)
[7] Story told in *Managing the Equity Factor*, Hussman and Hatfield (Houghton Mifflin, 1989)
[8] 1 Samuel 30:1-6
[9] Matthew 5:25
[10] Chris Novak, *Conquering Adversity* (CornerStone Leadership, 2004)
[11] Matthew 11:28-30
[12] I Corinthians 2:9
[13] Matthew 7:8
[14] Galatians 6:9
[15] Matthew 5:5
[16] Romans 9:38

CHAPTER EIGHT – OPTIMISM
[1] Matthew 5
[2] Philippians 4:6
[3] Luke 8:9-15
[4] Matthew 11:28-30

CHAPTER NINE – POSITIVE CHANGE
[1] Max Dupree, *Leadership Is an Art*, (Doubleday, 1989)
[2] Exodus 4
[3] Genesis 12
[4] Galatians 6:9

CHAPTER TEN – EMPOWERMENT
[1] James Belasco and Ralph Stayer, *Flight of the Buffalo* (Warner, 1993)
[2] Exodus 18:23
[3] Luke 9:1-6
[4] Luke 8:22-53
[5] 1 Peter 4:10
[6] Luke 9:10

CHAPTER ELEVEN – COURAGE
[1] Judges 7
[2] Genesis 6-7
[3] 1 Samuel 17:37
[4] Acts 9:23-30
[5] Acts 4:1-4
[6] Acts 9:20
[7] Luke 4
[8] Romans 12:2
[9] Charles Swindoll, *Hope Again*, (Word, 1996)
[10] Isaiah 40:31
[11] 1 Peter 4:12-16
[12] 2 Timothy 1:7
[13] 1 Peter 4:19
[14] Hebrews 10:35-36
[15] Hebrews 11:25

CHAPTER TWELVE – EXAMPLE
[1] John 13:15-17
[2] Matthew 7:12
[3] Luke 11:52
[4] Matthew 15:14
[5] James 3:13
[6] 1 Corinthians 4:16
[7] Titus 2:6-8
[8] 1 Peter 3:15-16
[9] 1 Samuel 12:23
[10] Galatians 5:22-23

CHAPTER THIRTEEN – PREPARATION
[1] Ephesians 6:10-17
[2] Psalm 119:105
[3] 1 Peter 5:7
[4] Mark 1:35
[5] Romans 1:11-12
[6] Matthew 28:19-20
[7] Mark 6:30-32
[8] Proverbs 17:22
[9] Romans 12:3
[10] Luke 9:12-17
[11] Luke 8:22-25
[12] Luke 8:26-39
[13] Luke 8:43-48
[14] Luke 5:17-26
[15] Luke 5:12-15
[16] Mark 6:45-52
[17] Matthew 9:27-31
[18] Matthew 9:33
[19] John 11:1-45
[20] John 2:1-11
[21] Luke 22:49-51
[22] John 5:1-16
[23] Hebrews 11:6
[24] Ecclesiastes 3:1
[25] Psalm 25:4-5
[26] Proverbs 3:13
[27] Isaiah 6:8

CHAPTER FOURTEEN – THE ULTIMATE VICTORY
[1] 1 Corinthians 3:11-13
[2] Ecclesiastes 5:10
[3] 1 Timothy 6:17
[4] 1 Corinthians 4:2-5
[5] Ecclesiastes 12:13-14
[6] Matthew 7:16
[7] Psalms 103:15-16

ABOUT THE AUTHOR

David Cottrell is president and CEO of CornerStone Leadership Institute. A nationally known public speaker and business leadership consultant, Cottrell has trained more than 120,000 managers at major corporations and has been a featured expert on public television. He is also the author of 18 books.

Prior to founding CornerStone, Mr. Cottrell was a senior manager at Xerox and Federal Express. He also led the turnaround of a Chapter 11 apparel company – National Spirit Group.

He can be reached at:
> P.O. Box 764087
> Dallas, Texas 75376
> 888-789-LEAD
> www.CornerStoneLeadership.com
> david@CornerStoneLeadership.com

Other Books by David Cottrell available at
www.CornerStoneLeadership.com
> *12 Choices … That Lead to Your Success*
> *Monday Morning Leadership*
> *Monday Morning Customer Service*
> *Monday Morning Communication*
> *175 Ways to Get More Done in Less Time*
> *Leadership Courage*
> *Management Insights*
> *Listen Up, Leader*
> *Listen Up, Teacher*
> *Listen Up, Sales and Customer Service*
> *The Leadership Secrets of Santa Claus*
> *Becoming the Obvious Choice*
> *136 Effective Presentation Tips*
> *Birdies, Pars, and Bogeys: Leadership Lessons from the Links*
> *The Manager's Communication Handbook*
> *The Manager's Coaching Handbook*

A MESSAGE FROM THE AUTHOR

Dear Reader,

I believe with all my heart that Christian leaders can make a difference in our society. The purpose of the book was to provide you a guide as you search through the Scriptures for the answers to today's issues.

It is my sincere desire that the principles expressed in this book will help you become a more effective Christian leader.

In addition, my desire is for this book to be the vehicle to expose as many people to Jesus Christ as possible. During the next two weeks you will have the opportunity to recommend this book to at least ten friends and associates. It will inspire your Christian friends and reveal the wisdom of the Bible to your associates who do not know Christ. Your recommendation could make a difference!

This book was written for a selfish reason – I needed to confirm that my leadership teachings were Biblically sound. Through the course of my journey, I found that the answers to all our questions are in the Bible ... and it does not take a Biblical scholar to understand God's word ... it only takes our wanting to hear. This has been a rewarding and faith-building experience.

May God bless you,

David

Recommended Reading:

12 Choices ... That Lead to Your Success is about success ... how to achieve it, keep it and enjoy it ... by making better choices. **$14.95**

You and Your Network is profitable reading for those who want to learn how to develop healthy relationships with others. **$9.95**

Monday Morning Leadership is David Cottrell's best-selling book. It offers unique encouragement and direction that will help you become a better manager, employee and person. **$14.95**

Conquering Adversity ... Six Strategies to Move You and Your Team Through Tough Times is practical guide to help people and organizations deal with the unexpected and move forward through adversity. **$14.95**

Leadership Courage identifies eleven acts of courage required for effective leadership and provides practical steps on how to become a courageous leader. **$14.95**

Leadership ER is a powerful story that shares valuable insights on how to achieve and maintain personal health, business health and the critical balance between the two. Read it and develop your own prescription for personal and professional health and vitality. **$14.95**

Management Insights explores the myths and realities of management. It provides insight into how you can become a successful manager. **$14.95**

The Ant and the Elephant is a different kind of book for a different kind of leader! A great story that teaches that we must lead ourselves before we can expect to be an effective leader of others. **$12.95**

Visit www.CornerStoneLeadership.com
for additional books and resources.

☑ **YES! Please send me extra copies of *Leadership ... Biblically Speaking***
1-30 copies $19.95   31-100 copies $16.95   100+ copies $14.95

Leadership ... Biblically Speaking   _____ copies X _____   _____

Additional Leadership Development Resources

12 Choices ... That Lead to Your Success	_____ copies X $14.95	= $ _____
You and Your Network	_____ copies X $9.95	= $ _____
Monday Morning Leadership	_____ copies X $14.95	= $ _____
Conquering Adversity	_____ copies X $14.95	= $ _____
Leadership Courage	_____ copies X $14.95	= $ _____
Leadership ER	_____ copies X $14.95	= $ _____
Management Insights	_____ copies X $14.95	= $ _____
The Ant and the Elephant	_____ copies X $12.95	= $ _____
Biblically Speaking Package	_____ packs X $119.95	= $ _____
(Includes all of the items listed above)		

Shipping & Handling $ _____

Subtotal $ _____

Sales Tax (8.25%-TX Only) $ _____

Total (U.S. Dollars Only) $ _____

Shipping and Handling Charges

Total $ Amount	Up to $49	$50-$99	$100-$249	$250-$1199	$1200-$2999	$3000+
Charge	$6	$9	$16	$30	$80	$125

Name _____ Job Title _____

Organization _____ Phone _____

Shipping Address _____ Fax _____

Billing Address _____ Email _____

City_____ State _____ Zip _____

❑ Please invoice (Orders over $200) Purchase Order Number (if applicable) _____

Charge Your Order: ❑ MasterCard   ❑ Visa   ❑ American Express

Credit Card Number _____ Exp. Date _____

Signature _____

❑ Check Enclosed (Payable to: CornerStone Leadership)

Fax	**Mail**	**Phone**
972.274.2884	**P.O. Box 764087**	**888.789.5323**
	Dallas, TX 75376	

www.**CornerStoneLeadership**.com

CornerStone
Leadership Institute